WRITING OUR WAY

A Supplement for Students in First-Year College Composition

William L. Knox
Northern Michigan University

KENDALL/HUNT PUBLISHING COMPANY
2460 Kerper Boulevard P.O. Box 539 Dubuque, Iowa 52004-0539

Contents

Part III Supporting Your Writing

Preface

Once a fellow teacher said that textbooks are for teachers, NOT their students. He said students didn't read them anyway, but teachers learned as they taught from textbooks.

I don't really believe either case is absolutely true, but I confess that composition teachers were less in mind than composition students when I started this slender and less-formal book. I imagined myself talking to composition students in a kind of experiment, suggesting they engage in a kind of "composition conversation" with their friends and classmates and you. Each after all can claim some ownership for texts—the individual student's writing "my way" is really an "our way" once connections in writing communities become clear. Only later did I consider my "conversation" extending to you as well.

This informal text, having suggested itself from my past teaching and writing, will encourage your students to ask more of themselves, their writing classmates, and you. It recommends that they understand the first-year writing course, participate in class, ask questions, and meet you for conferences. I don't expect you as a fellow composition instructor to agree with all my observations and methods here, but I hope you will recommend this book to your students as a supplement that can help them improve their writing by meeting you halfway.

Throughout the text encourages critical thinking, dialogue, and writing as a way of learning. To this end you will find my advice to students in the three sections about getting in touch with themselves as writers, talking about writing, and supporting their writing. This book shares my experience as a teacher and student of writing as it asks students to be reflective about themselves as writers, to become self-conscious about what goes into their writing.

What you won't find is a total treatment of the subject. That's for you and your students. I have tried to show, without much apparatus or heavy explanation and definition, how students can be better writers in their college milieu, actively approaching your course with them, balancing solo and collaborative writing.

Each chapter has WRITER'S MIRRORS, places inviting students to write, maybe for the first time, about their writing alone and in community. You may make these WRITER'S MIRRORS assignments for class discussion if you like, but consider permitting students the freedom to offer their responses on their own during conferences and workshops.

Please recommend this short book along with the rhetoric, handbook, and reader assigned in your course to help students to find their own way beyond their textbooks as they break away from the experts to discover their own processes, need for improvement, and voice.

In the end, I hope *Writing Our Way* will make your teaching more lively and your students' writing more substantive and fluent. Most of all, I hope this book will show students what they all must do at the end of a course: leave us, their teachers, behind.

I Hear Your Protests: A Few Words to Open

As a first-year college student, you will probably write a lot—more than you're used to—in your first writing course. You may have to brace yourself to spend lot of time and to seek help in a RE-QUIRED course, one apparently having nothing to do with your major. You may be tempted to do as little as possible, to wrap it up as one-night stands, and hope for the grade you need.

But your writing coursework—some that may push you to the edge of your ability or endurance—deserves more attention since it is practice creating meaning in your personal, academic, and later professional life. This lightly written book can help you find ways through composition to open you to recreating your everyday world on paper and to take some of the frustration out of making sense of your new college study.

The best way to make this kind of sense is to realize that you are not in this alone, that the best writing often balances the personal with the collaborative. Throughout the book I address YOU as an individual writer, but only to have you consider the WE in your writing course: the direction you—that all-important "I"—can find as a writer from your instructor, classmates, and others as well as yourself. Recognizing and asking writing help from others is not a short-cut—this text does NOT encourage you to have others do your writing for you. Instead, you are asked to realize that any writing you do is done in the context of people: For a long time you may have thought, "I write MY way!" when in fact you could just as easily have said, "I write OUR way—because my teachers and classmates influence my thinking and writing."

Reflection and action will help you to use this influence to your best advantage. The most important thing I know about writing successfully is the educated guess I share in this book: the more aware you are of the *what* and *who* and *when* and *where* and *how* of writing, the easier and more rewarding the process and results of your writing will be.

I wrote this short book to show a bit about what I have learned from teaching and observing the work of students and teachers. My intent is to make the job of writing easier and clearer for you, your classmates, and your instructor. Success in writing isn't always a matter of having high test scores, or reading a lot of books, or even writing till you slide under your desk. What's important is being straight with yourself about your writing processes and products, accepting their messiness and the need for community.

Instead of exercises in logic, rules telling how to write-or-else, assignments to turn in, or even readings by big-name, published writers, you will find advice from a guy who has always struggled with writing, who never learned how to type, yet who knows that reflection on and activity in your writing environment will help you to be a better writer before the end of the term.

In the chapters that follow, you will begin to see how the writing job opens itself and opens new possibilities of language and community that can work FOR you.

Give this slender book a chance to push out your personal writing edge. Think of it as a GUIDEBOOK through your first-year college writing course, even as a part-time companion to learn with—and one who will never hit on you for vending machine quarters!

Carry *Writing Our Way* along with you to the library, friends' rooms, dorm study lounge, shade tree—anywhere you study and write. Just hop in anywhere and find advice about getting your college writing done in a way that works for you and your classroom audience while you cruise through the other curricular (and extracurricular) necessities of college life.

Remember that *Writing Our Way* asks you to lose some of your innocence, however, by encouraging you to get proactive in approaching your instructor, sharing your work with your classmates, and closely examining your own process of writing.

Sometimes college writing is going to make you want to scream, get crazy, and throw things—like your roommate. These desires are sometimes normal responses to the frustration of putting words on paper, for professional writers as well as someone who is just starting. But instead of making a spectacle out of yourself or risking arrest by the campus police, use this book to help focus your protest and energy to find a writer that's you.

I hope *Writing Our Way* refreshes your sense of self as a college writer, shows you how to make some learning choices, and acquaints you with the value of writing for improving all your college work. Good luck!

Part I

Getting in Touch With Writing

Maybe you didn't write much in high school or maybe you wrote every week. In either case, chances are you will write more papers in your first year composition course than you imagined. In these first four chapters, the focus is on activities only you can initiate to get in touch with yourself as a writer.

The relevance of the first, **"Doing Writing Assignments,"** may seem obvious, but it asks that you broaden your view of what "doing" and essay and being "done" means. If you think of yourself as a "nonwriter," then **"Developing Your Writing Process"** may show you how to build methods to fit your composition class. **"Improving by Saving"** shows how reviewing your past writing can change your writing habits and self-perception. **"Creating a Writer's Notebook"** invites you to construct writing materials from your class for your benefit. Each of these chapters is intended to ease you down the way toward thinking of yourself as a writer, by writing, by seeing the writing you've done in new ways, and by recognizing the importance of teachers and classmates in your writing.

Chapter 1

Doing the Writing Assignments

The first two sections of this chapter will help clarify when you are DOING writing and when it is DONE for the class deadline. It will also show how hasty writing helps neither you nor your teacher. In the two sections following, suggestions will be made for improving writing processes.

Confusing "Done" with "Doing"

DOING assignments and having them done sound simple but these two terms often collect many and sometimes conflicting meanings. That's why we start here. Doing the assigned work in a class has a material sense in terms of PRODUCTS: one has to write papers, take quizzes and tests, and submit papers to earn a grade in the course. The first-year writing course is no exception—one has to submit products such as essays, notebooks, and tests, to earn a mark. Stress on writing products remains a large part of writing assessment and grades, but there is more to writing than the neat deadline drafts.

Too often writing students will "DO" assignments focused only on the deadline essay to get the grade or because it's "what the instructor wants." Too seldom an essay is submitted for the writer's LEARNING—to make meaning, to practice writing processes, and to write responsibly for an audience.

HOW writing assignments are completed addresses the PROCESS, the DOING, of learning by writing. In reality, many student compositions that are "done" have barely begun: there is a typed paper but little has been learned about how to create meaning on paper.

Students will sometimes say they are "doing" an essay before anything is written because they are THINKING about it. Others will say they are "done" with their writing when the first draft is written in their notebooks or pecked out on computer disk. I ask that they both move ahead a step. Although thinking is essential, I recommend to the first student that it is better to THINK and WRITE together to begin testing meaning on the page. For the student who says he's "done" when the first draft is on paper, I suggest that he has just STARTED because only now can he SEE the words, JUDGE them, and REVISE toward the deadline draft.

Knowing When Looks Aren't Everything

Sometimes beginning writing students believe that doing a paper means some time sitting at a desk, or table, or word processor, concentrating on producing a paper that LOOKS neat or, preferably, like pages out of a book. Sometimes much thinking, drafting, and word processing is channeled into having a centered title, regular margins, and five-space paragraph indentations—into arranging right-angle lines on a page as the apparent focus of their essay. Typewriters and computer printers do that already; however, your contribution is really bigger and not always as neat.

Whatever time or thinking or formatting you spend to make an essay neat, it is by the act of putting pen to paper and fingers to the keyboard that an essay becomes on the scratch-work page or computer screen. This is the point where any writing is born but also the point where it can die. In the face of a deadline, such matters as how grades are given and how the heading is positioned can cause stress about how writing product is seen by the instructor. (Sometimes this stress is voiced as "Does the teacher *like* me?")

Therefore, a "done" writing assignment is often identified with the final typed or printed, turned-in draft. The essay is "done" in a material, black-letters-in-straight-lines-on-white-paper sense. Too often this idea of writing is too tempting: Students are pleased because they can honestly say that they "did" a paper, it's off their backs, they're free for another week. Even some instructors are overly pleased when papers come to them in format and on time.

Like students above who believe that thinking means "doing" and a draft means "done," those who put appearance before the give-and-take of minds working on writing unwittingly delay their improvement as thinkers and writers.

Avoiding One-Night-Stand Writing and the Morning After

If writing is mostly an exercise in simply thinking or appearances, you can easily fall into the stressful pattern of putting off your writing until the night before when, after all, it may seem there is plenty of time (and NEED) to compose and to have the word processor make spelling correct and margins neat. However, latenight is seldom the time to do the best thinking or even to push the keyboard.

In another context, everyone today talks about the dangers of one-night-stands, of not knowing those who want to be close friends. Likewise, when you write a latenight paper, you may wake the morning after with doubts about the night before. An essay done in a rush is writing you don't really know, writing you may not respect, and writing that makes you wonder about the long-term effects on your academic life.

My point should be clear without pushing the comparison: just as it's a good idea to take time, ask questions, and get to know close friends, it's good to spend ENOUGH time with your writing to STUDY, to REFLECT, to WRITE, and to LEARN.

The one-night-stand approach to college writing contributes to a stressful pattern: Some teachers get writing that makes them want to throw things (like students) and to joke or click their tongues about about how "students today do only the minimum." As a result, they sometimes respond less to their students' writing and brace themselves for the next stack of unpolished, half spell-checked essays.

Students, too, can teach themselves to hate writing because it makes them stay up late, miss fun, and work-work-work. At worst, both teachers and students become unappreciative of the efforts of the other, so the whole enterprise of teaching and learning writing can disintegrate into elaborate paper shuffling whose only result becomes garbage in, garbage out.

At this point you may be thinking that I'm being very hard on student writers—and their teachers. I'm presenting an extreme view for purposes of illustration only. Now here's your chance to show what doing assignments means to you:

WRITER'S MIRROR 1.1

Take a minute here to briefly describe how you write an essay. Be honest: It probably isn't the way I've shown it above, but answer the important questions: How do thinking and writing work together? When do you write? What is productive and comfortable about your writing process?

_____

_____

_____

_____

_____

_____

Feeling Better About Writing and About Yourself

Whether or not you sense mutual yet unintentional teacher-student trashing consider another way of DOING an essay, one that begins with employing your interest in making writing work for everyone involved. Please ask: "What benefit could be in writing a paper for me? For my teacher? For who and what I care about?"

Doing an essay, really DOING an essay, means something external of course—filling pages in some regular way as you think—as well as something internal—learning about a SUBJECT, an AUDIENCE, and your WRITING SITUATION. At its best, learning writing means that in every composition you and your instructor can sense a difference in thinking, in craft, and in awareness of audience. Even if these differences aren't reflected in a higher grade every time on writing PRODUCTS, they will be reflected in your PROCESS.

DOING an essay really means writing to learn—a subject, ways of approaching the subject, and especially a set of individual and social work HABITS that will help you to see the words you write as meaningful action.

Such action takes several forms: it is symbolic action in the responsible words on paper; it is reflective action in your thinking, jotting notes, and writing; and it is social action in working with your teacher, classmates, and friends. Few students would think that the writing they do for a required class is social activity; maybe it's because they have been caught in the "garbage in, garbage out" trap for so long, ignoring their teachers and classmates who could make considerable contributions—once their presence and knowledge is no longer taken for granted.

Think for a moment about the relationship between your everyday community and your composition class. Classtime is taken from your day; assignments you do come from your writing teacher, your classmates, or you; someone—you—does them; and while you are doing the assignments you talk with others. Perhaps not directly and not all the time, but your teacher, fellow classmates, neighbors, friends, lover, and RA all can and do have varying degrees of influence on what, how, why, where, and when you write. Just as significant, you also stimulate them with your questions, with your answers, and with your ideas you express on paper.

You don't believe this? Haven't you EVER read a paragraph from your composition to a friend who smiled saying you were funny and you either shrugged off his response, wanted to make a face, or, thinking again, changed the paragraph?

WRITER'S MIRROR 1.2

Now take a minute to jot down what helps you to feel better about writing. How many of the things have to do with time? Teachers? With the right frame of mind?

_____

_____

_____

_____

_____

_____

Being aware in a systematic way of the things that help you DO your writing can point your way toward the important internal changes a writing class can encourage—observing closely the world around you, thinking more clearly, learning more through the process of writing.

WRITER'S MIRROR 1.3

Regardless of the positive roles others have in creating and responding to your writing, list now anything that blocks you when trying to write and think. How many do you come up with? How many of these are related to your college social environment?

_____

_____

_____

_____

_____

_____

To "do" writing, you have to be aware and master distraction so time spent on one paper will help the quality of thinking and language skills on those that follow—not just in your composition class, but in future ones, and in your career after college as well.

At this point, you may expect me to tell you how to arrange your college life. No way. I won't tell you to get rid of your stereo headphones, your moody boyfriend, or your crummy dorm room to go to the library, to get a life, and to word process your way to bliss. It's enough to ask that you begin, if you haven't already, arranging your life so you can write, say, a half hour a day wherever, however you best can do it.

Investing in Writing

Students sometimes tell me that the grade they get in their courses is their "pay" for the semester. I tell them they are partially correct since those ABCDE marks are meaningful in our system of socio-economic promotion—for getting credentials such as a diploma to start a career. (Grades disappear occasionally, at a few colleges, but seldom for very long.) I insist that the KNOWLEDGE and WORK HABITS students take out of the course are the real pay since these changes pay dividends long after they have left the writing classroom.

Writing courses like freshman composition are called service courses at some colleges because they "serve" all other academic departments by providing instruction in one of the most basic of all academic skills—written composition. Theoretically, a student who finishes freshman comp is ready to write term papers and essay exams. I believe, however, that the student who "does" her written work in the reflective way I suggest above, will be able to think, to plan, and to find greater significance in future coursework. When you really consider your writing, not just as an assignment but as a chance to refine your thinking ability, the real pay-off is clear because your "service" course can pay you interest in every other course and activity where writing skills are needed.

Yes, you are responsible for that final, slender, DONE essay: your name is on it and our college system seldom recognizes collaborative student authorship. But by understanding the possibilities in the surrounding learning environment, you can DO meaningful writing without the pitfalls of valuing thinking without writing, appearance without reflection.

Chapter 2

Developing Your Writing Process

✍   ✍   ✍

Just as a shift in attitude about doing writing assignments can get you started in a writing class, you can begin to adapt your composition instructor's writing approach to your needs as a college writer.

In this chapter, I'll provide some advice about writing and revision so you can think about ways to make writing less of a chore, more of a reward for you and others. Remember that the ideas in this chapter depend on giving yourself enough TIME and having enough ENERGY to follow through.

Finding What to Write ✍

Writing processes usually follow the leap-frogging stages selecting material, organizing these ideas toward coherent meaning, and finishing writing for a specific audience.

Although not always obvious, the writing process begins with your information and desire before you have a word on paper: You may have little information but a strong urge to write. Or you may be busting with ideas from reading and life, yet cannot put them on paper in an interesting way. Yet either strong desire or great ideas are good starting points.

However, even when you are neither excited nor informed, oftentimes you have to write anyway. If you are systematic in selecting information, then writing and thinking can be easier because you have support for your ideas—your interest will be evident to your audience. More important, drawing together information can be exciting as connections, not first apparent, between ideas begin to appear.

Using Personal Experience ✍

Material for an essay can come from two sources, depending on your instructor's assignments: your memories and reflection and publications and interviews drawn from class or outside of class.

Perhaps the most common essay students are asked to write is drawn from experiences—ones especially engaging when developed with classmates. Seemingly insignificant past events as well as present challenges—how you won your junior high swim meet or how you are taking on the campus financial aid office—may bloom into interesting topics for essays. One way to begin the writing job is to reflect in an organized way about your subject, jot down the important details, and consider the best ways to organize them into a coherent form. Organize according to time, space, or significance. Probably a topic that interests you will appeal to your classmates and professor who can help you to see ways to make it come alive. Try out the topic in class giving attention to the comments it invites. Once you have encouragement and helpful criticism, you'll probably be as primed as you can be to develop your ideas on paper.

Using Texts

Usually writing teachers assign textbooks, such as a collection of short stories or non-fiction essays to stimulate response to important issues. As you stick to these in writing your analysis or interpretation, you develop response unique to you while building with the ideas of others. For an essay of this type (perhaps about the influence of television advertising), good reading proceeds with good writing. Read the texts carefully two or three times until you feel you could sit and talk comfortably with a classmate about the views of the writers—better yet, talk with your classmates or instructor as a test of your understanding.

Next, make the meanings in the piece understandable by putting them into your own words, even if you find them difficult or distasteful or unpopular (perhaps the employment of images of family for non-family-oriented products). Third, try writing your ideas about your reading paraphrasing but also quoting the few most striking words from the original. If your instructor has given a specific assignment (perhaps to critique the position of an author), now would be a good time to discuss in detail your view of the reading and plan of organization and to clarify the intent of the assignment if necessary.

If you are using other published sources, whether they are books, periodicals (magazines), videos, interviews, and/or audio recordings, you should look first in general sources like dictionaries, encyclopedias, atlases, biographies, almanacs, and data bases to get a handle on a general topic you would like to pursue. From there, topics (such as "family" and "advertising") can be researched in the library electronic or card catalog, *Reader's Guide to Periodical Literature*, or any number of subject area indexes your reference librarian will help you locate.

Without a doubt, you must take great care to accurately quote, paraphrase, and summarize information from outside sources. Equally important is showing where you found your information using the Modern Language Association (MLA), American Psychological Association (APA), or other accepted documentation system. Your library has guides available to help you with the notation and works cited entries for these. Although record keeping about your information may seem annoying, without doing so you commit PLAGIARISM—using someone else's ideas, plan of argument, or key terms without acknowledgement. Sometimes students fail courses because of this easily avoidable oversight.

After you have written careful notes on cards or in notebooks—wherever—you should review this information a while, reading and rereading in your spare time until convinced you are thoroughly familiar with it and ready to begin organizing and composing your main idea or thesis. Again, even if your professor has not asked you to do so, you should try out your ideas on her to see if they fit the requirements of the paper you are about to start writing.

WRITER'S MIRROR 2.1

This is a good place to consider the advantages of drawing writing topics from both personal experience and from outside sources. List some ways these advantages affect your writing.

_____
_____
_____
_____
_____
_____

Drafting

Although notetaking and organizing continues throughout writing, at some point you will feel ready to begin writing the deadline draft. The first (or preliminary) draft may bear only a shadow of resemblance to the paper you finally turn in, but its finish, as noted Chapter 1 begins the real life of a paper. Doing the first draft is the time to pay special attention to where and when you write and to make the most of the time available until the due date. Whether it is your apartment, a cozy chair in the student center lounge, or a computer terminal, choose a place where you can work comfortably.

The importance of writing PROCESS should be clear in this chapter. Yes, the final product is concrete evidence of achievement, but you would do well to consider what you get beyond the mere relief of turning in the paper: a self-taught process that you can use again and again in your university years to meet the changing demands of your professorial audiences. Plan on leaving your writing course with working drafting habits that will beat the urge to fold when you're faced with the need to write.

It is best to write at least one more draft between the preliminary one and the deadline paper. Even if you work on a word processor, printing an intermediate draft to read aloud and to edit by hand away from the hum of the machine can improve "vision" of your writing to edit before turning in your paper.

WRITER'S MIRROR 2.2

Before seeing how "re-vision" might work, jot down your writing process noting ways it may have changed already since you read Chapter 1.

_____

_____

_____

_____

_____

_____

Revising from the Start

Revision begins with the earliest notetaking and scribbling. Just as you have a unique composing process, there is no one revision process. However, here are some possible helps if you have thought revision is only something for writers who have to correct their mistakes.

When you take your writing seriously, you have been selfconsciously revising from the start, revising from the first moment to consider the writing ahead. Scribbling and crossing out sentences, outlining and clustering, getting a friend's criticism, rearranging text on the microcomputer, and testing during writing workshops before the essay is presented all constitute possible steps in ongoing revision.

Revising After the Fact

Oftentimes revision is mistakenly considered the final obligatory stage after the instructor or class has asked for changes in content, organization, etc. The instructor may want you to edit the essay so that it is more in tune with the needs of the course or the conventions of academic papers. At this point, revision may seem merely annoying—after all, the paper has been turned in once already. But even this annoyance can result in learning for the next.

Revising Solo

If you are revising on your own while preparing a final draft, you must be honest with yourself above all else. Students often find it difficult to separate their egos from their work—the essay is seen as part of oneself and therefore difficult to see as something detached, as something in need of improvement. In order to revise, to become your own best editor, you need to look at writing as something detached from the self always subject to additional work. To begin revision, you can ask and then act on questions such as these:

- Is there any more I can say about the restricted subject?
- Have I tried to keep the interest of the reader?
- Are the ideas in the essay presented no sooner and no later than the audience needs them?
- Have I carefully reread the deadline draft for annoying errors in surface features?

Revising in a Writing Network

Remember though that you can pursue answers easily (and perhaps more profitably) to writing questions before the paper is presented. Students too often wait until the night before to get too "sick" of writing a paper to ask for help, to involve anyone else when they themselves are burned out. One characteristic of school writing process is this waiting for response after the due date by way of teachers' marks. It is better to get an instructor to make comments on papers beforehand.

And you know how to get this response beforehand: ASK.

When response to your essay comes before, you should carefully listen to comments about and completely read any written comments on the paper. Oftentimes instructors will write detailed responses answering most of the student's questions about the expectations of the assignment. By reading these carefully, you can save much time, worry, and effort. Of course, if the comments are not clear, you should ask the professor or TA for help deciphering them.

Even when all the marginalia makes sense, nothing prevents you from approaching the instructor for extra help. Instructors have ideas and idiosyncrasies that have to be understood. The resulting writing may be "what the professor wants" or, looked at in another way, writing for a specific audience. But to discover what a writing instructor really wants, students can ask critical, interlocking questions including:

- Is my material complete?
- Have I stated my main idea and developed it?
- Is the plan of the paper consistent with developing the main idea?
- Should I develop further?
- Is there other help I need?

Knowing answers to these questions is valuable in finishing the paper to the satisfaction of your academic audience and yourself. Not knowing answers to these questions, for whatever reason, can make writing tougher: remember that your instructors are in the business of helping you, so push gently for answers.

WRITER'S MIRROR 2.3

Review your revision process below showing its relationship to your writing process.

_____
_____
_____
_____
_____
_____

None of these observations about revision is bulletproof. At every stage in your composition, you have to put forth a good faith effort to communicate as clearly and as engagingly as possible. If I may return to the metaphor from Chapter 1, one-night-stand papers or any written without adequate time for research, reflection, and revision will usually meet with less satisfactory response ranging from a raised eyebrow to dripping red comments. Although sometimes tedious, revision can more often make a positive difference in the way an academic paper meets assessment and improves your knowledge along the way.

Making Your Move

You may be thinking by this time that you have heard or read a lot of this before, "Yeah, yeah. Think, read, write, rewrite, barf!" Regardless of the approach (or tricks) in the college classroom, you may perceive more of the same old English stuff you've had in high school.

WRITER'S MIRROR 2.4

I ask you to suspend judgment for a while and to think about your writing in a different light. What if we stopped thinking about writing as a product or a process, something to do or something that pays off to think of it instead of the other half of thinking? What then is the relationship between thinking and writing?

_____
_____
_____
_____
_____
_____

Thinking, like talking, is invisible to us because it's so transitory; therefore, we may not normally think of revising our thinking while revising a draft. When we write, whether it be a letter or an academic paper, we have the opportunity to become better thinkers by noticing how making changes on paper changes our thinking.

By writing we become aware of ourselves thinking as we run into problems and seek ways to overcome them. By writing we may suddenly become aware of a voice inside of us that says, "We're doing okay!" or "We're messing up!"—a voice not always heard.

In creating your own writing process, you are also creating ways to come closer to the thinking part, to the voice inside of you; it is for this reason that your writing process becomes, well, yours. If it's honest, it cannot be any other way: thinking and writing work together in conscious effort.

Above I outlined a number of possibilities for engaging your writing teacher, classmates, and friends. If you took this advice to be something etched on stone tablets, you've got me wrong. In this outline of possibilities, you still have to be the one to decide when, to what degree, and how each of the people mentioned above will be approached. You may be shy or extremely outgoing so your depth of involvement may be great or little. You may be socially assertive with your peers, but uneasy around teachers with all their degrees and books, so you try to avoid all contact except for an occasional question from the safety of your sixth-row seat or deep corner of the writing circle.

Writing and revision asks you to step out of this anonymity, to shed your former writer's skin for a new one, to allow yourself to talk to others and listen to the emerging writer's voice in you as it develops essay after essay.

Chapter 3

Improving by Saving

Simply forgetting an essay once it is done and turned in—especially if you have spent considerable learning time revising—can cripple your next. Keeping essays and looking at them from time to time can help you to see where you have gone as a writer and thinker—and how far.

Facing the Past

When I was an undergrad, I confess, I almost never looked at a paper immediately after a professor returned it—never looked at except for the quick flip to the back page to see the grade. After that, I may as well have tossed it out my dorm window because, if I didn't slam dunk it in the circular file, I crammed it into a notebook never to be seen again.

To tell the truth, though, I almost always eventually got around to going back through my papers, reading my professors' comments about content to see if I "got it down" or not. However, I seldom if ever looked at the sometimes painstaking corrections in mechanics and grammar and, more important, the solid advice in the margins and at the end about point of view and rhetoric—the stuff that could perhaps have helped me to become a better writer sooner.

Enough of my confession though. What can YOU do with the papers you have written and had returned to you? Those blank except for a grade or laced, in vivid reds or purples, with ample expressions of your professor's knowledge (and sometimes obsessions)?

WRITER'S MIRROR 3.1

Jot down a short history of how you have handled academic essays returned to you. Tell the truth!

_____

_____

_____

_____

_____

Debriefing Your Essays

A good move with your first paper, one perhaps with only a grade, is easy even if it is a disaster: take it to your professor and ask for an explanation, in terms of content and rhetoric, of why you received the mark and comments you did. This is not a visit to a coroner's lab for an autopsy, but a walk toward a good opportunity, especially early in the semester, to see your professor in her office, to talk straight about what she can suggest to help you enliven future writing.

While in a writing course, you should meet your instructor to find out what this other experienced and professionally paid writer finds in your work and to learn something about negotiating meaning. By doing so, you prepare for the writing ahead.

The instructor who is open to these meetings, and maybe more informal ones over coffee or cola, can be your best guide to strengthening your writing before your college career progresses another semester. By the same token, even ask the instructor who consistently gives you good marks but writes little on your papers. I know the good grades look great even before your friends see them but being a good writer means improving your thinking to the point of knowing what usually works and what doesn't. Again, ASK your writing instructor about what more could benefit your writing.

You should never wonder if your prof or TA is carefully reading your stuff. As a student, you may make reasonable demands for helpful response to the writing you have put your hours of sweat and snacks into.

What about the paper returned to you covered with lines, circles, comments, and cartoons?

The first step is to try to figure it out yourself. Sort out where the instructor is providing constructive criticism and where he is merely making an observation (perhaps a humorous one). Frown and smile while rereading your paper the way she might have. Then if there is something specific—or many things specific—you don't get, make an appointment and talk about the paper, bracing yourself for perhaps a number of meetings, not only about the paper just returned, but the ones shared ahead in the course, too.

WRITER'S MIRROR 3.2	Write down an experience you have had talking to a writing instructor about a paper she's marked.

_____

_____

_____

_____

_____

_____

Hanging on to Those Essays for the Term

Regardless of how much or little your papers are marked, it is important that you hang on to them not just for the day until you understand where your instructor is coming from but for the term as well. Resist the temptation to throw them out of your dorm window in an orgy of celebration at the end of the week! Even without much solicited spoken response about your work from your instructor, these papers can still speak to you about your writing for the course because

- you can see what mistakes to avoid
- you can see your progress
- you can remind yourself of how "dumb" you used to be
- you can impress your friends with your filing system
- you can see for yourself that you indeed write and can write for the rest of the term!

Often for whatever reason, the human being thinks ahead not in terms of finding success but of avoiding failure. Keeping the papers for a class will help you to avoid the screw-ups that commonly result in lower grades on early papers. The first paper or two in the course will show if you need additional work in surface features like spelling and punctuation, grammar concerns like pronoun reference and subject-verb agreement, or errors in logic that reveal "beautiful" papers to be exercises in random access thinking. Likewise, you can look forward to greater success on future essays.

Depending on the skill and predisposition of your instructor, your essays will be marked emphasizing certain features of your writing while de-emphasizing others. One rule, one that I haven't tested very strenuously but nevertheless believe, is that by improving the features of writing made known to you by your instructor (and writing classmates) you also improve other features of your writing not shown to you. For instance, it's possible that if you improve transitions that overall coherence will improve as well. Because of our own learning, we will invariably evolve as writers even if no one ever assesses certain writing features—we make improvements in other areas, perhaps without a second thought, on our own.

In college settings, as you know, we cannot usually escape assessment. I think that is the best reason to hang on to all the papers you do in your writing class—to see for yourself the direction your writing is heading and to ask your classmates and professor what they SEE going on.

In class or in conference, an instructor usually finds it difficult to remember the features of your earlier papers—she may have only a single mark in her grade book for each one. But if you can bring a portfolio—a pocket folder or looseleaf notebook—of your papers to conferences, then both of you can read and speak intelligently about your progress.

Progress can be spoken of in many ways, the crudest is the letter or numerical grade. The specific ways in which your writing changes are better to address. When you see in essay margins something as simple as fewer marks for "comma fault" or as serious as "poor logic" as the course goes on, you know that something positive is happening to your writing. Even better is to read in blue at the end of the your essay, "Bravo! Your writing is much improved because...."

So each paper can measure your progress in meaningful comments. More important though are the improvements you see on your own.

The most subtle benefit of keeping your papers is proving to yourself, with each one returned to you, that you are a writer. If not in any other way, at least you can measure in thickness the stack essays you've written. Although this may seem trivial, nothing is more compelling than a record, a file of what has been DONE. One day two months from now, you may pull your writing folder from the shelf and surprise yourself at how much you have written and im-

WRITER'S MIRROR 3.3

Show what you have learned from papers you have kept and reviewed for this class so far.

_____

_____

_____

_____

_____

_____

proved.

I ask my students now to keep all the writing they do for our course as tabbed sections in a loose-leaf WRITER'S NOTEBOOK (see Chapter 4). Final drafts, preliminary drafts, and notes for papers add up in a hurry for the ten essays we write during the term. Even if your instructor doesn't require you to, keep a similar file to avoid the belief you're writing little for the course. Just pull out your fat binder full of your writing to give yourself a few strokes!

Hanging on to Your Essays for Life

Saving papers from week to week and from term to term can add up to your own book. I've always been impressed in some strange way by friends and colleagues who have saved their academic papers all the way back to their fifth grade *Robinson Crusoe* book report. But that doesn't always mean they share them. Saved papers, milestones of your thinking ability, can be embarrassing in public; after all, you're a better writer than you were just a month ago! Certainly you wouldn't want to bring them out on your first date, but that doesn't mean that they aren't important.

Americans often take photos and make videos of important events. These provide great humor in later years; but they also affirm the subjects were a certain way (flattering and not)—wearing braces, making the winning point, or celebrating getting a drivers license.

When I look back on rough drafts of papers I've written, I sometimes try to deny to myself that I ever wrote them, but I'm happy, too, for the progress I have made, the evidence of which I sometimes share with students and friends. Yes, I ask myself how I could have been so messed up to write that strange *Clockwork Orange* research paper, but I also ask myself where I would have been had I not learned from those drafts that helped me to write better in the future.

I'm still very self-conscious about my writing, and in a lot of ways I'm not as good as I should be; but I am better than I was because of invaluable self-coaching that would have never happened if I hadn't studied my earlier writing.

Papers affirm our intellectual life above all else because they are often the only tangible evidence we have that we have learned anything at all in college. (Have you ever tried to review your learning with an old computer scoring test form?!) Your old essays may be awkward and only occasionally brilliant, but you need them to know where you have been and where you would like to go.

Launching a Portfolio

Increasingly, colleges are looking at new ways to assess their students' writing abilities. Over the years, placement and proficiency tests, lower and upper division writing courses as well as English and major field writing courses have all been tried to get a fix on the writing ability of students like you.

A newer development in this now common game of standard assessment is the portfolio. Generally, a portfolio is a compact collection of a person's work done over a period of time. Art fields have used this approach for years to assess student work as well as professional work done by artists, designers, cartoonists, and advertising graphic artists.

More specifically for student writers, the portfolio can be assembled in various ways. Some professors use these now to assess student writing at the end of the term. These are usually composed of a representative sampling of writing, usually the best efforts. Portfolios of student writing done in several classes are already being used for assessment at some colleges. The papers may represent work in English as well as major field writing classes.

Keeping your papers in the form suggested above gives you a running start in the direction of a portfolio if your school requires one or if it decided that it may in the future. Although colleges seldom change the graduation requirements for its already enrolled students, who knows what the future holds—you may be able to catch the wave!

Chapter 4

Creating a Writer's Notebook

✍   ✍   ✍

The essays you save can start a WRITER'S NOTEBOOK. This chapter will examine how various kinds of writing that you may take for granted can be even more valuable if kept. Personal observations, reading and listening notes, class notes and teacher's handouts, and drafts of your papers can enhance your writing performance when maintained and studied.

A writer's notebook can improve your fluency and improve your perceptions about writing because, unlike the alternative of not keeping your writing, it's a concrete record of your performance in class. A writer's notebook can be thought of as a diary or journal for personal thoughts and observations. For our purposes, however, I would like you to think of a writer's notebook as a less than private document in terms of its sources and audience. If your writing teacher has asked you periodically to submit a journal for to review, you may already accept that a continuous record of your writing will be seen by others.

Beyond this idea, think of assembling a writer's notebook from a variety of sources: notes from reading you do, notes you take in your writing class, and preliminary and deadline drafts of papers you write, classmates' essays from workshop activities, your instructor's handouts, photocopies of source material for essays, as well as the events of your personal life.

Remembering Personal Experience ✍

Oftentimes students are hesitant about a highly personal approach to essay and journal writing—to be sure there are others who enjoy this diary approach and achieve success once they get started. Part of the problem for the first group of students is that they do not make the distinction between writing about "private" as opposed to "personal" experience.

"Private experience" I define as the highly unusual, possibly embarrassing (or even potentially incriminating) events and deep feelings that one would rather keep unsaid and especially unwritten. "Personal experience" I define as the everyday social life. From time to time something really interesting or significant comes along that makes everything else seem like a waste of time, too. Generally speaking, personal experience is anything you would feel comfortable having a conversation about. When this distinction is made, you may see that you have much that could be written and shared with others. The highly private stuff in the context of a class is perhaps best left inside our heads where it can be relished or eventually forgotten.

What use is there to writing down personal experience? The answer for me remains simple and it is an answer much like the answer I give to other areas of writing: it gives us "room" and time to practice writing. Apart from space and time issues, writing about personal experience challenges us to recall and to put into written language events that might soon be forgotten or, through the crush of new memories, become blurred.

WRITER'S MIRROR 4.1

Think for a minute about some events you wish you would have recorded—now jot down a few. Maybe these weren't the most earth-shaking or may even seem "stupid" to you now, but wouldn't it at least be fun to look them over again? Moreover, by writing them down you will see something about the way you handle written language when NO ONE is putting the slightest bit of pressure on you with due dates and assignments.

_____
_____
_____
_____
_____
_____

Reconstructing Your Listening and Reading

Recording secondhand experience—the events that friends relate to you or ones you simply overhear in the cafeteria—is good practice for a writer's notebook since there is no risk to your ego as there may be when you record personal events. What you write down has already been shared and can promote your commentary—interpretation—in writing to go along with the events shared. Sometimes I ask my students to simply write a conversation they had the day or night before to see how much they can remember and to see if they feel the same way about the conversation. Oftentimes even a short interval between event and writing changes our interpretation.

Like secondhand experience from speech, secondhand experience from reading is something worth recording as well. I had a professor once who, as far as I know, never read without a legal pad next to him to write down what was significant. I have often wondered how big his NOTEBOOK LIBRARY must be!

By writing down ideas and impressions, he could pull notes for lectures, presentations, or conversation. Consider the value of a journal with notes on your classroom and personal reading. You would be ahead of the game in your classes and you would have a record of stuff you feel was important to read. Of course, I know what you're thinking, that this kind of notetaking takes TIME that is already in short supply. Granted—if we are looking only at value for the present moment. For quizzes, hourly exams, finals, and, yes, even essays, however, you would SAVE time by reading dozens of pages you have written instead of rereading hundreds written by someone else.

Furthermore, by copying, paraphrasing, or summarizing stuff from textbooks and from your own reading, you are learning, remembering, and restructuring your thought about the subject matter. Chances are the material will stay with you longer; you will in fact have learned better.

WRITER'S MIRROR 4.2

Take a moment to scribble down what kinds of first- and second-hand experience may be useful to you as a writer in this class.

_____

_____

_____

_____

_____

_____

_____

Keeping Class Material

I have some experience seeing how other composition teachers teach their courses—some invariably lecture, others simply ask students to write, others, like me, talk about writing in a less structured way while helping students in groups and as individuals. Looking back over notes from my undergraduate English classes, I wrote down almost as much stuff that I found witty or interesting as I did the course ideas I thought I was "supposed" to write down. A writer's notebook can also be a record of what your writing teacher has to say about writing and life and those things she may especially think significant in your writing as a student. When students tell me that my minilectures go over their heads, I ask if they have allowed themselves the opportunity to consider class words in the privacy of their thoughts outside of class; in short, I ask if they took notes.

Unless electronically recorded, spoken words exist for the moment and are gone, often not to be considered again because there is nothing to remind us of them. Even if you jot down a few of your writing teacher's words each time your class meets you will have a leg up on writing in general and your writing in particular. Remember, too, to jot down what your classmates have to say. In a writing workshop everybody can be a teacher and you can find help by everyone who sees your writing and speaks to it—if you take notes.

Also good to include in a writer's notebook—either with class notes or as a separate section—are the instructor's handouts. The course syllabus, reading lists, assignment sheets, sample essays, exercises, quizzes and tests, etc. tell their own story about your course. Apart from reading them occasionally to follow the class schedule, you can also find clues about who your instructor is and what she expects of you.

WRITER'S MIRROR 4.3

Show how you keep class notes and handouts. How useful are they in this system?

_____

_____

_____

_____

_____

_____

Preserving Preliminary Drafts

Of course, early drafts are great to include in your journal because so many of them are false starts and rewrites. These papers stand as a living record of the way you think each time you write a paper, of a long-term process, which at its best, shows your growth in literacy skills and imagination.

I encourage my students to keep ALL of their early drafts whether they are handwritten, typed, or computer printed. This makes their writer's notebooks bulky, but I insist for a number of reasons: First of all I ask students to keep them since I like to look at the evolving processes they use during the term. Often during the term, not surprisingly, my students write neater, fewer drafts of succeeding essays because they are getting experience with words on paper. I like to see this but intro comp students NEED to see their increasing efficiency and effectiveness as writers.

Second, these early drafts, especially the ones abandoned for lack of interest or information, serve as raw material for papers later in the course or perhaps in a course they will take later. There is no guessing the time saved by students who have notes to draw on when their interest or new sources of information open to them about a topic they once began.

Third, these old drafts, often written over by the writers and annotated by their classmates and me serve as record of thinking at work, of several minds meeting to address a common search for meaning. What are the results of this reminder of several writers at work? I hope that the trace that's left demonstrates that time wasn't wasted, that the work done in writing class isn't simply a kind of academic one-night-stand, that they have come out of the experience better writers, better thinkers, and more appreciative lovers of writing.

Cherishing Deadline Drafts

Just as important as preliminary drafts are the marked deadline drafts returned to you by the teacher. As I said in Chapter 3, these "final" drafts serve as the public record of your best writing effort. The record of how well they were received is tangible evidence of how your writing holds up to audience response after you have run out of ideas, energy, and time—when you have met the deadline. Sometimes during writing conferences, teachers like to return to earlier papers you have written; keeping them in the writer's notebook makes sure that you can produce them when asked.

Much good writing instruction today is done by teachers and students sharing each other's writing for response. What better way is there to make your work available for the response of your instructor and classmates than having it altogether in your writer's notebook? As a teacher, I appreciate the ease with which my students and I can talk together about writing when it's all in one place. During writing workshop, my students often have their notebooks open working alone or sharing their drafts with neighbors.

The writer's notebook is not simply another assignment or exercise; it is an unobtrusive measure of what you do in a writing class. The measure is much different from the ways your essays are assessed. The writer's notebook holds an almost complete record of everything you have done in a college writing course. It may not be neat with pockets and dividers (although these help), but it nevertheless is a file that shows your approach to and the results of your writing in your course.

Even if your writing teacher does not require you to, please keep a writer's notebook as an aid to learning about yourself as a writer involved in a complex learning process. If you are a person whose idea of neat is "hanging" clothes on the floor so they won't fall down, fasten all your composition-related paperwork into a binder anyway to keep it in one place.

A student of mine—responsible about her work, employed on campus, developing clear career goals—once showed me a writer's notebook that looked like a gerbil nest. Yet among the odd-sized crumpled paper, parti-colored drafts, and overlapping sections, a story of her as writer emerged, showing me that neither her process nor final papers required any apology.

And neither should yours.

Part II

Talking About Your Writing

Implied in the title of Part II is the social dimension of writing study. The four chapters above have asked you to consider talking to your teacher and classmates about your writing while building the record to do so. The next four chapters will show you ways that a variety of people—often closeby—can be the best resources for writing your papers. Teachers, the most obvious, will come first as the chapter advises about reasonable relationships to foster. The next chapter will suggest how your classmates, those sharing the writing classroom, can be your allies. The writing center will be recommended as a place on campus to get additional advice. Finally, those who I broadly define as your neighbors can provided help as unexpected as the writing center's is easily found.

Chapter 5

Asking Your Teacher

The Numero Uno person in your college writing life—after you, of course,—is your instructor. We'll look at who a writing teacher is, how the advantages of talking together can help, and what a conference can do.

Considering Your Writing Teacher

It may be helpful for you to begin by finding out who your writing teacher is. As a rule, writing instructors are easy to approach, and yours probably is, too. But you may want to examine your assumptions and briefly take a look at your writing teacher before making your move.

She may be a graduate student trying to earn her way through school. Perhaps he's a part-time instructor who makes extra money teaching. Maybe the young assistant professor is, just like you, learning the ropes at a new school this semester. Or maybe you have a salty old prof whose years teaching has drained him of all vitality except for reserves of cynicism—or more likely the best writing advice you'll EVER get.

Chances are your college comp instructor doesn't fit any of these stereotypes but is someone with a life full of interests and one of them is the study and teaching of writing.

Perhaps teaching writing as a career or even a job seems like a strange occupation to you: you may figure that she is simply doing a job or slumming in academia or filling up a teaching schedule while waiting to be assigned to teach literature courses. The truth is (and I hope it is a big truth) that most college writing teachers teach first-year comp because they want to help you become a better writer in the three or four months you're together. The activities that she plans, the time she spends discussing writing in class, the eyestrain she endures reading your essays, and the suggestions she offers for writing improvement speak to the interest she has in you and in improving herself in this part of her profession.

Some writing instructors will take every reasonable opportunity to talk to you about your writing. I've known TAs and professors alike who turn chance meetings in hallways and at the indoor track into lively academic discussions. Any student can usually shoehorn a minute or two after class. If you show interest in your writing, then you'll be welcome to talk regularly about your writing.

Sometimes, however, writing teachers become frustrated (sometimes noticeably) not so much with their students' writing, but with their unwillingness to talk about it. Students may very well ask, "What is there to talk about? I do the paper, hand it in, and get a grade!" Such response may be appropriate in classes where the teacher mostly lectures about rhetoric, literature, current events, or anything else in the name of teaching writing and then collects essays once a week. Few lecturers, however, will ever ignore a student's willingness to learn when she asks questions, makes observations, and shares examples of her writing.

But another type of writing teacher believes writing is best learned by writing and by talking about writing and then writing some more. The difference between these two types of teachers often confuses students, so it may be good to look at how something positive can be gained from both.

Generalizing Writing Teachers Some More

Let's look at two general types—one, who lectures about writing, gives assignments, grades them, and gives them back to you; the second, who provides classtime to write and who is often on the scene encouraging your best performance by example, advice, and assessment.

If you have lecturer, you may be pleasantly surprised at what happens if you show up at his office hours one day to ask for his advice on an upcoming essay. Don't be put off by a frumpy or spiky exterior. I'll never forget one intimidating, top-down, prof I had as an undergrad who was fearsome in class and who frankly asked me in class one day if my major paper final draft was "a joke." I had made the mistake of not approaching him before the paper was due to avoid the error of my untutored ways. But I did go see him after my public humiliation (and measely defense) to ask him what I could have done.

Almost at once, our relationship relaxed—though too late to have much effect on my grade. Not only did he show me something about dictionaries and research, but also we talked to each other about my plans for going to school out east (he highly approved), the state of the English teaching profession that I hoped one day to enter, and many other things, showing that I could talk, that he was a human being, and, if nothing else, that a reasonable learning relationship could be established in those few weeks before the end of the term.

In short, the writing professor who enjoys lecturing is probably concerned about your writing and willing to review your work for improvement. Unlike my example, be sure to get his attention early in the term.

If your writing teacher is the second type who conducts writing workshops and is already open to your writing and willing to talk to you about during classtime, then you may have already easily learned that the stuff you put down on the page can have much to do with the words voiced in the air, the relevant (and often irrelevant) topics that are created and pass between two people who are interested in the construction of knowledge—words written on paper.

If your writing teacher is open during class time, pursue him (within the limits of reason and social propriety) to talk about your writing and his. (Yes, talking about writing is a two-way street.) Even quiet teachers will enjoy the time you spend together working in meaningful ways toward making sense in writing.

WRITER'S MIRROR 5.1

Describe your relationship with your current writing instructor. Contrast expectations with reality.

_____

_____

_____

_____

_____

_____

Learning to Do Together

If you've read earlier chapters, you know the ways that your writing instructor can help. Unfortunately, in classroom settings, students are sometimes so lulled or intrigued by the words from their teachers that they forget that these teachers have ears, too, that can listen to what students say about their writing. Teachers then will respond, in particular, to what students ask and say about their writing. You know that a writing teacher talks to you in traditional lecture and question-answer classes. Beyond that we know that in writing workshop classes teachers make the rounds—often turning classes into miniconferences—briefly reading and talking to students in their small groups, I have encouraged you as well to approach your teachers after class with questions. Out-of-class student-teacher conferences, too, create favorable situations for discussing writing. All of these count as ways of studying writing together.

Being Assertive in Writing Workshop

When you find yourself in a writing workshop class, you can get the most out of it by doing what cannot be as easily done by simply raising your hand or seeing your professor after class. Writing workshop time is time to share your writing with your classmates and teacher. Unfortunately, your teacher is only one person in a class of twenty-five students. In a regular fifty-minute period, you get less than two minutes—unless you are ready with something to show, ask, and say.

Too often, students are content to let their instructor give a quick glance and a "That's fine" to their workshop essays. Better is to have a ready question, one specific to your present work. Even under time restraints of the workshop, the instructor will spend more time engaged with the student who can identify a specific interest in the paper at hand than with one who simply nods. Even the most jaded, I've-seen-it-all writing instructor responds to students who are intellectually wide-awake about their work.

Making Writing Conferences Work

During outside-of-class conferences in particular, teachers can respond to student writing in helpful and personal ways if the student takes the initiative. Having your instructor respond to writing during classroom workshops should be normal; having her respond to your work without the distractions of the classroom and with fewer time constraints should be rewarding for both of you.

No "typical" writing conference exists, but there are some common features. Before even opening your notebook, get comfortable in your prof's office. Find a place to sit, spread out your papers, face your teacher or sit at her side. Glance at the bookshelves and walls. Situate yourself so you feel that the office is your turf, too.

A good way to start talking is to address the essay you're working on. Better yet, arrive with the last several. If your teacher requires you to keep your work in a writer's notebook or on a floppy disk, bring that along so you can review performance over several assignments.

Once you have a subject, then you are in a position to talk about it. A professional weakness of teachers is talking too much—professing sometimes may seem to get out of hand. Although you have come for advice, make suggestions yourself following from your instructor's remarks. Sometimes students will sit and simply say "Okay" to everything the teacher says. This is not dialogue; the opportunities of the meeting are lost without it. If you understand, repeat back what was said, scribble notes, suggest another alternative. If you don't understand, say so and get on with the business of making meaning in your essay.

Sometimes you may have questions not apparent from the paper. Make sure you ask them; even write them down and take them into the conference with you. Sometimes your instructor will ask if you have any questions and it's okay if you don't as long as you're satisfied that the two of you have made the best possible use of the time you've had together.

If necessary make a follow-up appointment. If individual conferences are a regular feature of the class, then agree on an agenda, a list of issues to talk about next time.

Returning for More

While writing your drafts, it's a good idea to bounce your ideas off your professor again and again, but not fawningly or excessively. Remember that you are not really alone when writing and that response to your work does not have to wait for your deadline draft at the late-night mercy of your professor's bloodshot eyes and even redder pen.

Often the most important lesson in a writing class is the unexpected one that shows your writing coming into being when students and teachers compel themselves to talk about what's important. Surprises are desired by many writing teachers, but they don't have to wait to be pulled out of solitary composition—they can pop up every day a writing student and her teacher focus on some new writing.

WRITER'S MIRROR 5.2

How do you use time talking to your writing instructor?

_____

_____

_____

_____

_____

_____

Revisiting Teacher and a Student Who Did

Let me share an example. Once a student, who I'll call Jennifer, took me at my word and showed up in my office about two days before each paper was due. And she came armed: in addition to the draft of her paper, she brought a photocopy of it and a clipboard. By the end of the first meeting, we established a routine to follow at least twice a month for the rest of the year: I would read the original of her paper aloud while she annotated hers.

It was great fun talking about her essay, the sources of her ideas, her goofs, and my misreadings. At the end of fifteen and often thirty minutes, she had marked her paper, we were satisfied with the results, and strengthened a valuable professional bridge between us with each meeting. I would return to the work on my desk, and she would go play her favorite net sport, typing her paper after she had a bit more time to polish it.

Her regular appointments with me benefited both of us. She learned that my game was to help her to be the best writer she could be and I gained valuable insight into student writing process and how I could be involved in it.

Considering a Possibility

A quick word of warning: some writing teachers, no matter how stingy or open they seem, are never satisfied.

Let's say that you get up the stuff to talk to your writing teacher for the first time, and when you do, you're told that you should try something else, a new topic, another approach, more specific detail, or even a new life.

Even if your professor says that you should try something else, get tough and try challenging him with another way into your topic that may be more pointed.

One way to gain the respect of most writing instructors is to demonstrate your compelling interest in the topic you are writing about and your ability to approach it in a critical way. If more research is needed, read more. If the approach is wanting, consider other possibilities of the ideas at hand. If it's the topic you don't want to address, ask for another shot at it giving it the fire or cool that it needs.

Some students may call this "jumping through hoops" or "kissing ass," but don't believe it for a minute as long as you're satisfied that the teacher is working with you, to pull out new meaning, to make you aware of the legitimate possibilities of English prose in narrative, analysis, argument, or whatever form. As long as you feel you are being encouraged, energized, or vitalized, why don't you think of your negotiations as writing for a specific audience and maybe, in the long term, even for a friend.

No matter who your writing teacher is, chances are you will find out much more about how she can do her job, about how much she can help you create meaning, if you take the initiative. Talking to a writing instructor doesn't have to be like contact with an extraterrestrial; on the contrary, it can be the one close encounter that introduces you to the best any college has to offer: meaningful dialogue between students and teachers about issues that count.

Chapter 6

Sharing Writing Classrooms and Classmates

✍   ✍   ✍

College writing classes, the places where you write papers and meet your instructor and classmates, can be lectures, discussion groups, or workshops. As you know even without reading the last chapter, classrooms are largely reflections of the instructors who lead the classes, but in this chapter I want to focus on your relationships with your classmates.

WRITER'S MIRROR 6.1

What kind of writing class activities are done by you and your classmates?

_____

_____

_____

_____

_____

_____

Maybe this question comes at you too soon. Maybe you haven't been in class long enough or maybe it defies easy label drawn from your experience. But at least you have a starting point for understanding how you interact with your writing classmates. Now let's look at the various kinds of writing classrooms with an eye toward two goals: first, to identify the kind of classroom you are in, and second, to consider ways you can conspire with other classmates and your teacher to recreate your classroom activity to improve your learning.

Asking More from Lectures   ✍

One kind of college class is the lecture in which the professor mostly talks about writing for the better part of four hours a week.

Student participation is usually limited more than in the workshop discussed below, but this time-honored method can work for students interested in active learning. During this time you take notes about writing and are provided with the opportunity to ask questions. I do not believe this writing classroom is common today. If you are in one of them, you may have to make the most of the opportunities to work with your classmates and teacher about writing outside of classtime (as shown in Chapter 5 and below in this chapter and Chapter 8). But there are opportunities of another kind.

This type of classroom runs on the teacher's considerable knowledge of writing, so by taking careful notes and paying close attention to examples, you should apply these ideas and write good prose essays for the professor or one of TAs according to the terms outlined in the class.

If you do as you are instructed, you will probably get good marks. You may have to channel some of your initiative and imagination in writing practice but you can learn writing skills by principle and example.

If you are not willing to sit, listen, and write, you have two avenues to take more control of your writing: the first is to take full advantage of the question period(s) during each class to clarify and to ask about options that you can use to build your knowledge. For instance, if the instructor says that you should follow the example of Hemingway's tight prose, you might respectfully ask how far that notion should be taken for the current assignment. Even better is reading an excerpt of your own work to use as a basis of comparison with what is asked for.

By asking, you will have the benefit of immediate response from the professor and will encourage other students to do the same. Students may even lead the discussion of writing in helpful directions not previously considered by the instructor. In this small way, you can take some charge of the lecture period and help your fellow classmates—even if it means taking chances and sharing ideas.

A second way to approach lecturing professors is during their office hours (again see Chapter 5). The conference is a time when you can have the undivided attention of instructor. She may even be happy to see a student take initiative to make an appointment or just drop by. During this time you can get close attention to your work by individual response. (It was during one such meeting when I as a sophomore that I got enough good advice in one hour about writing and developing a thesis statement helping me through the next three years of college!) Consider also the possibility of taking along a classmate who shares your writing questions.

Whether in class or out, make your questions substantial and clear. Listen to what the instructor says and try to follow good advice. Don't hesitate to ask more follow-up questions. And remember that the questions you ask are probably in the minds of your classmates; usually you will not be the only writer to benefit.

Writing More in Workshops

Perhaps your writing classroom is a workshop where the instructor is open to your working and sharing ideas. Writing workshops are characterized by a large degree of openness, collaboration, classmate reading and response, and professorial guidance instead of directive. Although the instructor "guides" your writing invention in some way, perhaps by providing "trigger" exercises to stimulate your thinking, you largely follow your own initiative writing and reading journals, bringing in writing to work on during class time, and searching for (or hiding from) the advice of your instructor. Assessment is usually based on the terms of the papers written with respect to how well they develop a sense of audience, purpose, writer's persona, and content.

You eventually make accommodation with your writing classroom method and your classmates. Like the lecture, the writing workshop provides you with opportunities—usually more than the lecture—to write, to consider options, to receive response from peers and professor during classtime, and—in short—to write and learn by doing.

WRITER'S MIRROR 6.2	Describe what kinds of classroom activities would make you a better writer.

_____

_____

_____

_____

_____

_____

Learning with Your Classmates

Take a minute to look around at the people in your classroom. These are your classmates, your peers—not just various generic people occupying chairs, not competitors—they are diverse human beings who are sharing the struggle to improve their writing. They are, in various ways according to their talents, resource persons who would be happy to talk about their writing. You may have to take the initiative to approach a classmate to begin a new relationship; at least you have to be open when another takes the initiative in your direction.

In the writing workshop use opportunities to talk to your classmates about your work. Sometimes you may have to wait your turn in your group, but students who work diligently in workshops often get writing done faster, on topics central to their concerns, better than they could under the lecture system.

The best feature of the workshop is that it allows dialogue in the classroom between you and your classmates. You can share ideas, swap essay drafts, and arrange to meet after class as some of my students have done. Writing workshops have great potential to get your ideas into the air where your classmates openly discuss them with you. At the very least, you can complain about how tough writing can sometimes be or avoid the writing difficulties experienced by others.

I know some of the problems with workshops. Students don't always use the classtime well—sometimes the coming weekend makes for hotter dialogue than the essay about financing next year's tuition or imagining a world without pollution. Peer criticism may not be critical enough. Too often a "That's great!" starts and finishes a classmate's response for a paper you REALLY need help with. Some students can't write or "open-up" in workshops, claiming the need for solitary time to compose and revise their work.

In spite of these concerns and others, you can use writing workshops to write, get response, and, if nothing else, get the bulk of the writing done during classtime making the class a, well, writing class instead of a listening or snoozing one.

WRITER'S MIRROR 6.3

What are the limits on your talking about your writing with your classmates? Explain how these limits hurt or help your writing.

_____

_____

_____

_____

_____

_____

Writing Your Way (Plural)

Schooling can isolate and divide students, putting them into competition with one another, hindering learning. Reflect for a moment about times when you and your friends have studied together and how helpful it was. Now imagine doing the same during classtime. The circle of writing students can make a difference for those who make a good faith effort to use the time moving writing forward.

Of course, the classroom scene is initially filled with almost all strangers. Learning about your classmates and becoming effective co-learners takes some effort. Here are some ways to get together with your writing classmates.

The first step of involving your classmates in writing discussion is losing your fear of showing your writing to others. Let your new writing classmates pause over your sentences in a way impossible if you simply read to them. Recently I lost my fear of leaping from the high diving board after not having done it since high school. After taking the long plunge myself (and watching friends do so), my fear left. Sharing one's texts is the best cure for fear of an audience— after the first, the next opportunity almost seems natural.

The second step is specifically identifying those you would like to work with. Sometimes this is the same group or groups you join in your class workshop. A circle of four to six student writers can work together for a whole term learning to relate as writers. Even if the groups change from week to week, you learn how to edit with a variety of people. If you choose your own groups day-to-day, you may quickly fall in with a group that will decide to stay together all term. Regardless, you should try to identify early on classmates you can work with.

The third step of forming a writing group is to talk about writing regularly in class workshop, avoiding too many days when you choose to "pass." Insist also on meaningful response from your classmates. Although assignments vary from teacher to teacher, if you and your classmates can choose assignments that are important to your everyday or imaginative life, you will find classroom talk much more compelling than it would be about lowering the drinking age, abortion, gun control, or some other chestnut.

You must stick to writing and speaking truthfully and respectfully of a classmate's work. Demand the same from your writing partners. Any of the steps above is worthless if someone decides to be Conan the Critic with his classmates' writing. Look for ways to give responsible criticism without slips into exaggeration or sarcasm and don't take spurious responses from anyone else. One joy of writing class is that no one has to be in competition with anyone else—everyone can improve together if everyone contributes.

Writing Your Way (Singular)

One thing no one can do for you is make the day-to-day decisions about what you'll do in a writing class. Regardless of the kind of class you have (and I repeat, the descriptions above are over-simplified at best given the variety out there these days), you are the one who makes it a success or not.

At all costs, find the characteristics of the course that work the best for you and go with them. If your classroom provides time for writing, use it. If you have to sit listening to the umpteenth lecture glorifying the rhetoric of the ancient Roman Cicero, do it—but remember that your reading of contemporary essays and books shows that this ancient didn't have the last word on style. If you and your classmates spent time in class simply talking among yourselves about writing, fine—make sure you have new writing to talk about.

At the root of all of this is the hope you do not simply have to endure your writing course. Not even the most recent developments in teaching writing appeal to every student. New waves, propelled by recent studies in the teaching of writing, have achieved wide acceptance in recent years and are now the standard writing classroom approaches. But they won't cover all the bases—no system ever does.

So make sure that you talk to your classmates. See where your composition class takes you, even if it's in the direction of finding help outside of the classroom. With the advent of writing centers, conference teaching, and especially computers, the trend may be away from centralization anyway.

Chapter 7

Visiting the Writing Center

Outside of your writing class, you are free to meet anyone to ask questions about your writing. You may want to consider visiting your campus writing center for help from trained writing tutors. This short chapter will discuss what a writing center is and how to get the most from the help it offers.

Hesitating for No Reason

At once I want to put aside the stigma attached to visiting writing centers: they are not for lousy students but for any who have legitimate questions about their writing. The student (and sometimes faculty) bias against writing centers at some colleges is based on the plain wrong assumption that these places are for "stupid" writers or anyone dull who didn't "get it" in class. Nothing could be farther from the truth: writing centers are for students who need help with writing—even accomplished students find advantages going for a second opinion about their writing. This may seem like a paradox, but many writing teachers believe students who need them the most visit them the least.

Regardless of your writing ability or level of performance, the writing center staff member can be your best professional writing friend next to your writing instructor. Maybe even a better one in some ways because unlike your courses where university computer put you—you walk into the writing center on your own or are specifically referred by your writing instructor. In either case, you show up because of frank problems in your writing that you have not been able to talk about or resolve along with your writing teacher.

Asking About the Writing Center

Before writing and learning centers, students could only go—officially—to their teachers for help. With more open enrollment policies, many colleges found that writing centers answered the needs of students with educational backgrounds that had not adequately prepared them for college writing.

Over the last couple of decades—yes, a long time—writing centers have grown within colleges and universities to help students over the rough spots and often rocky roads of writing. Usually centers are staffed by learning specialists, teaching assistants, gifted undergraduates, and full-time faculty who talk to students one-on-one about their difficulties and offer everything from a quick fix like proofreading to comprehensive assistance with invention or writer's block.

Finding Your Writing Center

Your campus may not have a place called "The Writing Center" but a "Learning Center" or other place where students can get help with a variety of subjects from reading skills to math to computer programming. At some colleges these larger centers combine writing, reading, math, and other skills to reduce the cost of individual attention. Probably your campus is like many where there is a Writing Center staffed by tutors and equipped with microcomputers to provide help specifically with student writing. Regardless, the writing center staff on your campus provides usually free help that you can use in whatever way you see fit. If you have trouble with spelling or if you just want to discuss the organization or controlling image in a piece of your work, a tutor on the writing center staff can help.

As with visiting your writing professors, time during a writing center appointment is important. Depending on the week of academic term, the amount of time available with a writing center tutor may be practically unlimited, like in the first several weeks, or almost impossible to get, like at midterms or finals. Although it is not always possible to work ahead, if you need help at the writing center, bringing in a draft early can help you establish a "regular" time or at least make your needs known, perhaps helping to get an appointment easier in the future.

Unlike visiting your professor, the Writing Center staff will not know you or your work the first time. They will have neither positive nor negative predispositions toward you. You will have to explain where you are in your writing and ask for the help you need. It may be the case that you may find the help you are getting is different from what you thought it would be. This shouldn't come as a surprise—as we know, talking about our writing often changes it and our thinking about it.

Writing centers, depending on the size of their staffs, hours of operation, or just as a matter of policy, offer service by walk-in and/or by appointment. It is usually better to find out the phone number of the campus Writing Center to make an appointment. If you just happen to be cruising by, though, it doesn't hurt to try to see a tutor as a walk-in.

A very important point: always bring along a paper, one in progress or one just returned. Better yet—as in the case of going for a faculty conference—bring along your writer's notebook. Just as meeting your professor, a meaningful conversation about your writing is impossible without a sample of your writing in front of both of you. If you have one that the teacher has marked, your tutor can have a better idea of the standards and foibles of your professor and based on these can help you with a rewrite or with a draft of your next paper.

However, showing up with just a rough draft is fine, too. Just come with a text to discuss.

In either case, be ready for the tutor to spend some time reading your work, studying it, and asking some questions to explain the expectations for an academic paper, to decipher your handwriting, and to ask what the assignment was. Every time, it's most important that the Writing Center tutor have a clear idea of what it is you are to write. If the topic is left up to you, then you should acquaint the tutor with the other requirements that your instructor deems important. If there is a specific assignment, it is best to bring the assignment sheet or your notes from class the day the assignment was given. Often as a tutor, I listened while a student unsuccessfully tried to recall the assignment so we could begin to work on it. Students who are clear about class requirements usually give tutors—and themselves—a head start.

Working with the Writing Tutor

But once work begins with reading and talking about your writing, try to be as open as you can to the special needs of the tutor. She may ask questions or spend long moments in silence trying to find a suggestion that will help you write better. Don't let the silence make you uneasy. Thinking is the business of people in colleges and often we sit and do it together.

Writing tutors are great people to talk to about your writing. In the semi-private setting, you can learn another point of view about your work from someone who sees your work with fresh eyes. Your tutor can sometimes see knots in your work that you and your teacher may miss. Whether the problems are simple—punctuation—or tough—coherence of ideas—your tutor can aid you in finding solutions.

You should not expect, however, the tutor to do your work for you: his job is not simply to fill in the stuff you mess up—to proofread your work and scribble corrections for you to word process away. The best tutors will show you ways to become more independent from their help by suggesting ways to study and other resources. In the end you will become a better writer, taking responsibility for your work and relying on more usual channels of help—your instructor, classmates, and friends.

Sometimes tutors get criticized when, after still getting low grades on his writing, a student blames the tutor who "said the essay was fine" just before it was turned in. Tutors are people, who, like instructors and classmates will respond to a text as long as they receive response from the writer. I have never known a tutor who did a student's work for him and hope I never will. It is always YOUR essay: you are responsible for understanding the assignment, developing your voice, and proofreading the deadline draft.

Leaving the Writing Center Behind

You will reach a point of diminishing returns when you and your tutor realize that the Writing Center can provide you little more help, that you are on your own as writer no longer requiring the special services offered. Be honest with yourself at this point: cut the cord and move on to a less formal network to talk about your writing. If you have come to the center for remedial help with surface features and grammar, then you can use a handbook to get the quick answers you need when your ability "slips." If you came for help with invention, structure, research, etc., then take away the habits developed in your private and group tutorials and practice them on the next assignments when they're needed.

Maybe the best way to look at a Writing Center is as a place where you get the tools to grow your own garden, not just enjoy a quick bowl of salad. The short-term intensive help you receive isn't meant to continue indefinitely; it begins, lasts a while, ends—but is available again should you need further help. Just as you don't need (or want) your former drivers ed teacher in the car with you now, you don't need a writing coach at your elbow every time you write either.

As with your writing teacher, you need to ask for the help you need, but you need to go your way eventually, combining your knowledge and skill with the solid advice of others.

If you campus has a writing center, take advantage of it when you need the extra-professional help a trained tutor can provide. Don't forget, however, those sources of help closer to home: in less institutional surroundings, anyone interested in your study can provide immediate and often personal writing help.

WRITER'S MIRROR 7.1

Even if you have never used a writing center, what is some additional help you would like to have with your writing?

_____

_____

_____

_____

_____

_____

Chapter 8

Asking Others Who Care

In some sense it's easy to see that your writing teacher is a person to talk to about your writing. After all, she is your teacher. By the same token, it may be just as easy (if not more so!) to stop in your Writing Center to find ways to improve your work. It's also relatively easy in time and space to talk to your writing classmates around classtime. But it is also easy to forget that many other people would willingly suffer with and celebrate your writing. They may live closeby—down the hall, across campus, around the block, or across the country, but if you don't already know who they are, you can discover them with little effort.

Even with the current interest in collaborative classroom learning and writing classroom workshops and help from instructors and centers, much of the college student writer's work remains to be finished outside the classroom, even outside of easily identified academic settings. Seldom, though, do students or teachers consider the importance of this non-school space and time since they are perceived as unstructured and often less productive by both teachers and students.

Although, it can be argued that students often have ample opportunity to try out their work on their peers and professor during classtime, nonclassroom writing time can be more interestingly structured in your interests if you recognize opportunities for sharing knowledge about writing.

Some help, as we have seen, presents itself in the form of the Writing Center and conferences with writing TAs and professors. Other help though is closer in terms of psychological, geographic, and social distance.

In this chapter, I'll share some suggestions for the most comfortable writing advice you can get. Some of it comes from the most interested person of all—yourself. Your classmates might be more helpful outside of classtime without the crush of the class hour. Your campus friends and neighbors and even professors from other courses may surprise you. Finally, even your family can offer advice and a very special kind of criticism.

Finding Your Strengths

Just a word about the closest "other" of all. You can be your own best aid to writing during moments of uncertainty by remembering the most useful writing lessons of your past schooling. Former teachers, even less-loved ones or those who taught classes other than English, provide much needed help etched in your memory that you may recall. Not all remembered lessons are useful ones such as "Never start a sentence with 'And'!" but reflecting on the common sense lessons of writing can help a student when she feels that she knows little. More than once, a "ghost" from my past has reminded me to make a logical connection or get more information for a paper.

Also, we can be sharp when writing learning opportunities present themselves. In listening and reading, we often pick up turns of phrase, new ideas about sentence and essay structure, and new ways of thinking about writing process. When we hear and see more than just content, we begin to understand better how language can work. If you have a way to remember, to file these away, to make them your own for future use, then you are being your own best writing friend. If you're not sure how to use a semi-colon or make a neat transition, your reading will provide PLENTY of examples when you LOOK for them.

The world is so big we can never cover it all, however. Since we are social creatures, usually it's to our advantage to talk about writing with others we see as a normal part of life because it's more interesting and more fun to share our questions and miseries and joys with others.

WRITER'S MIRROR 8.1

What are your informal strategies for finding answers to writing questions?

_____

_____

_____

_____

_____

_____

Approaching Writing Classmates Outside of Class

As shown in Chapter 6, our writing classmates can be a source of help during class meetings; moreover, there is nothing to prevent continuing your writing conversations outside of class. One simple way I encourage my students to reach out to each other after class is publishing a class directory (with names and telephone numbers, other information is optional) at the start of each term. With this system, students are only a phone call away from each other for help that ranges from getting the assignment to meeting for some mutual writing, editing, and proofreading. (If nothing else, swapping jokes about your teacher's outlandish outfit that day can relieve enough tension to get a writing assignment started.) Even without a class directory, you can make your own directory of classmates' phone numbers.

Occasional phone calls are fine, but the best out-of-class relationship would be a semester-long one in which classmates regularly get together to talk about their writing work, to share ideas, and to try out their work on each other.

I ask you to imagine time well-spent with your classmates in a library study room, in your dorm room (or apartment), or even cafe reading each other's essays, talking about them, and exchanging criticism. You and your classmates working together outside of class create a powerful force for what can happen inside classrooms during workshops because other students see your improvement and something more—how easily you can talk about your writing, a sign that you "get it."

Another change you may see is improved assessment of your collaborative writing. Your writing teacher may be interested in your arrangements for out-of-class work as a model for encouraging other students. Most writing teachers prefer to have their students earn good marks on papers and portfolios; they appreciate students who go the extra distance to make their writing work. But even if you cannot find classmates who are interested in these advantages to working together, you have an option to those who are closeby in another sense.

WRITER'S MIRROR 8.2

What are your informal strategies for talking about writing class after hours?

_____

_____

_____

_____

_____

_____

Involving Neighbors Down the Hall and Across the Street

As a writing student, you can enter mutually helpful—and satisfying—relationships with other students who live in your building or in your room or apartment. Sometimes you may seek help unconsciously by just leaning across to your roommate asking, "How does this sound?"

Neighbors, especially those in the residence halls, can provide quick aid for writing questions that pop up while you are writing in your dorm room. Asking students you already know from seeing on your hall, in the cafeteria, or in the lounge, you may find them willing to loan their ears, eyes, dictionaries, or word processors for help with your writing.

Some always seem to have some time on their hands and are willing to at least look at your essay believing you will do the same for them sometime. Although you may not know someone really well, you may be surprised how willing relative strangers are to help out each other.

Reading and commenting on your writing is the most obvious but also risky way to ask for another opinion. You have to be willing to, first, share your work with a stranger, second, ask for her time, and, third, brace yourself for a possibly unwelcome "No!" Seriously, though, it takes guts to let relative strangers read your writing. You may take your instructor for granted, your classmates mutually interested, but neighbors—even if they're friends—with a grain of salt. Nevertheless, you will be able to tell how helpful they are by their seriousness, willingness to talk, and tone of voice. You can exchange favors with those whose comments get results; you can avoid those who are too quick in their reading and too flip in their response.

A less threatening kind of assistance comes from reasonable borrowing of writing tools. Asking a friend for a better dictionary, more powerful software or word-processor, or even quieter room may give you a leg up in your writing. Students typically share their experience and stuff in residence halls; it is not unreasonable to borrow and to loan the stuff that may help academic work. I knew a student who had free use of his roommate's electronic typewriter. Late nights, he would jam along on his papers, heavy metal on his earphones, lights off, writing more and maybe better than he would otherwise.

Learning from Other College Instructors

Alert students also pick up the sometimes not-so-subtle lessons that other university professors and TAs provide by design and accident. When professors in non-composition courses ask for papers, they will sometimes devote classtime to writing instruction—even if it is just a matter of outlining the paper requirements. If not, they often make themselves available for conferences about term papers outside of class. Almost every professor and TA has his/her idea of what an academic paper should look like and often these characteristics can be carried over into your regular writing classes. Sometimes, professors even supply outlines or models of term papers; these could be learning aids to you as well.

As an undergrad, I learned the most about writing in the shortest time from my American History TA mentioned in Chapter 5. The half-hour we spent after a test review session helped me not only on the essay portion of the midterm exam but also in every assignment I had afterwards. Writing help might come from sources you least expect!

Even Asking Family

With the ease of light-speed telephoning and high-speed travel, even parents can be a help. I have had students who have read parts of their compositions to patient mothers hundreds of miles away. Sometimes parents or siblings have special writing skill so they can act as tutors. Even if family members cannot provide specific help to you, they do provide an audience opportunity for your paper, moral support, and evidence that you are doing something academic at college.

WRITER'S MIRROR 8.3

What are your informal strategies for talking about your writing with others who can be helpful?

_____

_____

_____

_____

_____

_____

You should never feel that you're the only one who has writing to do or that there is no help. Oftentimes it's only a matter of asking the people closest at hand. Also writing students should not forget that talking about writing is mutual—the help you get you may be asked to return to a student who knows even less about writing than you think you do.

As a writer, you work in a community that even though largely unrecognized is filled with people (including you!) who have knowledge about writing that is ready to share. This is your writing community: some of it is easy to see in your instructor and the writing center. The rest, you may have to work for to develop, finding those who are most helpful, realizing all the while that the responsibility for writing rests principally with you.

Part III

Supporting Your Writing

In the first section, this booklet has stressed the importance of writing, talking, and thinking in developing your compositions. In the second, commonly shared settings and people you find there—classrooms, writing centers, dorm rooms, teachers, tutors, class-mates, friends, and family were emphasized to show the wealth of assistance you can find and return.

In this last section, the emphasis will largely focus on what you can do apart from the usual academic dimensions of writing study to become a better collaborative and individual college writer and thinker. In these last four chapters, settings, time, hardware, and your memory of your present composition course all explain this paradox in creating writing that will serve you and the writing needs of your community.

Chapter 9

Finding and Owning Writing Settings

In terms of producing text, the places you write can be almost as important as any knowledge and help you gain. Perhaps you never think much about these places—we are as unaware of them as the micro-circuits in our wristwatches and word processors. They are places we usually take for granted—the desk in the dorm room, the library table, our sprawl on the living room floor. Yet your writing place along with writing time are two factors often identified by students as conducive to or interfering with college writing.

Being There Already

You may be one of the lucky ones. Perhaps you already have well-defined study habits from high school and therefore immediately develop the kind of environment you need whether it is the kitchen table or carrel deep in the college library stacks. You may know already whether or not you need the peace of the library or the click of keyboards in the computer center or the shuffle of hundreds of students cruising by you on the cement walks of the college grounds. If you know, then you are fortunate to act and to get on with the private part of writing. If you don't know, then you might find the suggestions in this chapter to be helpful.

Finding a Place from Somewhere Else

Sometimes we come to a college writing class with no clear idea of how to provide ourselves with a good place to write; often your writing classes don't cover student writing environment. It may be the case that like many of college students, you had your room at home with a desk or bed and stereo so you could create your kind of writing place.

I can imagine such a place: Your paper in the drawer. Your typewriter on the desk. The sounds of your favorite CDs? Right there from the stereo. The writing assignments may have been tough, but at least you could count on the comfort of familiar surroundings with the necessities at hand.

Maybe you were in the another, less private situation where your writing place was at the kitchen or dining room table close to your mother doing the dishes and your kid sister watching reruns on cable television. Although less private, you may have adapted to this arrangement through elementary and high school and did reasonably well—the household distractions not withstanding.

But, moving to the present, you may be sharing a 12 × 12 college residence hall room or and apartment with someone whose taste in music and values in personal hygiene do not match yours. Maybe the campus scene has not yet shown itself as supportive of studying and writing as it has to the sometimes overwhelming spontaneous social distractions. In spite of the conflicting needs to read, write, and think, maybe you can find and make places responsive.

Keeping Social Needs in Perspective

New college students are often torn between the need to get their academic work done and the need to be with their friends or to do personal stuff including work and hanging out, so they work out often interesting compromises that succeed to various degrees. Some of these are introduced here.

Maybe a bunch of friends from the same writing class agree to study together in an apartment with munchies and music. Here you can set up territories on the carpet, enjoying collective messiness and camaraderie. If everyone agrees to spend time writing for a couple of hours, they have the benefits of other listeners and readers. This may be a better way than class workshop in the early stages of a draft to get response to the ideas and effects you compose—even if the responses are sometimes irreverent!

Another writer, however, may prefer the company of just one close friend with their books and papers mingled on desks, chairs, and futons. Whether this friend is an intimate acquaintance or a no-nonsense classmate, the caring comments can be more compelling, informing, and educating than from those interested strictly in writing.

Others may opt for going as a gang to the library and occupying a study room or table together. Study rooms are especially fine private areas where students can spread out their drafts, dictionaries, and other resource materials. Writers can read their drafts aloud, argue, punch away on notebook computers—anything they can do at their apartment with the added advantages of library resources just outside the door.

The quiet of a table in the open library compels you to work at a whisper when jotting down ideas. Whether alone or in a group, library composing can be influenced by the study atmosphere, one that encourages focused effort. A study carrel, too, gives you the advantages of the library along with a private writing table during lengthy reading and writing. More pleasantly, a carrel next to a window overlooking campus can provide much needed eye relief for those hardball writing sessions.

Other possibilities, less inviting at first glance, may be places where you find composing waiting to happen. As an undergraduate, I finished a lot of writing surrounded by friends in the TV lounge of my dorm. You may prefer the hustle and clank of dishes at your campus center coffee shop. Others may choose their kind of writing background noise from places limited only by the architecture of campus and community—the part-time job store room or the fifty-yard line at the stadium.

Whatever your choice of the moment this semester, you have to make these places and arrangements work for your writing. You can ask your friends for response to your writing. But have you ever tried to write while your friend chomps down some chips? Or type while lying on your stomach while your friend dances to some postmodern music three feet away?

One difficulty with group writing usually isn't the place but the social arrangement that can quickly shift into distraction and amusement. Often the place to write has to be one where, at least for a while, you have some degree of psychological isolation even if it means using tough vocal or body language to help others understand your needs. At the risk of reading like someone in another context, sometimes it's best "to just say no" to social commitments early in the weekday evening until you get a handle on your first draft. Try to achieve a balance between individual writing and group fun.

WRITER'S MIRROR 9.1

Write about your attempts to write with friends.

_____
_____
_____
_____
_____
_____

Finding A Bit of Space Here and There

The best strategy perhaps, especially if you have to rely on a choice of more or less public places—your shared apartment, dorm study lounge, library—is to find a number of places where you have space to use your writing hardware and the right kind of background sounds to concentrate. Taking full advantage of the variety, you will never have to count on using the library at midterms or your dorm during TV football night.

When I was a residence hall director, I marvelled at the way during a single evening and late night my student residents—toting their books, papers, and pens—moved from room to lounge, to library, to TV room, to fireplace room, to write a single essay. Perhaps this vagrant approach looks messy or procrastinating—and to some degree it may be—but it illustrates my notion that when you look you can find places that work for you as a writer—without going home to your parents' on weekends, writing in the basement because your little brother has taken over your bedroom.

In this era of options, you as a student writer should allow yourself the luxury of never being without a place to work—even if they are as different as the student center lounge and computer lab.

I know that word processing makes finding a composing place more complicated because—obviously—not every place you may want to work has a computer (and laptops can be expensive). But you should never believe that one needs a computer or a typewriter to think. Computers have been with us a very short time in the history of writing. Granted, I find myself addicted to writing final texts on my computer (as I'm doing now), but most of my writing has started on scraps of paper and napkins in coffee shops, on street curbs, and outside laundromats. From these humble starts, final texts can grow at keyboards.

Of course, being driven to the fringes of private or academic settings—with or without your favorite writing tools—is no replacement for a favorite place, one that you make your own.

WRITER'S MIRROR 9.2   Can you picture one place right now with the kind of environment you need to get words on paper? Can you think of more than one? Take a minute to jot them down.

_____

_____

_____

_____

_____

_____

Designing Comfort on Your Terms

As important as finding the right setting is making yourself comfortable. Even if we aren't rich and famous, most of us late-twentieth-century Americans are comfort-oriented—the right place means having the right stuff along and around. The right tape in the player, your writer's notebook, your old portable typewriter, the right stash of munchies in the bookbag, etc. Laying out our stuff around us identifies our territory and makes us feel at home even on top of a dorm washing machine.

My sophomore college roommate went to great extremes to redesign his half of our dorm room to create proper academic ambience.

Although he typed at his desk—and the typewriter was always ready—he brought in an upholstered swivel rocker, table lamp, hassock, legal pads, and even a pipe to help him compose his ideas. Sometimes he even brought in his latest squeeze to take dictation, too. I'm not sure much writing got done.

Having the right writer's stuff like enough light, plenty of pens, and a quality, paperback dictionary along can help improve any favorite writing setting. I wish I had a pizza for every time I was writing away from my desk when I remembered something I forgot—usually something insignificant like a fresh pen or the first draft. The whole purpose of having a good place to write is to be equipped and to feel comfortable there so the writing can get done.

Obviously, this is not snoozy comfortable whose fluffiness turns our writing to words spelled ZZZZZ. Allowing yourself to feel at home enough to lose yourself in (not consciousness of) your work may be an important part of doing a good job on the writing you do.

At home, the problem may be the reverse since you may have too many distractions close at hand. How many times have you gotten deep into some writing when suddenly the hum of the fridge becomes irresistible? When you see out the window you need to wash your car for later that night? When your pup wants to play? When the phone rings?

Yet these distractions can be diminished when planning is done. Often no one points out to college students that in spite of classes, work, and social responsibilities, they can reduce distraction at least for a little while by snacking first, going to the car wash later, leashing the pup outside, and switching off the telephone.

I have never created the perfect writing place for myself; however, I have come close—a dark room, latenight movies on cable TV, the only other light the glow of the words on my computer screen. Consider your own needs in terms of what is possible to achieve. Sometimes only the right background noise, that special roller ball pen, or favorite chair are enough. But consider, too, how a special writing place reflects who you are as a student and as a person with connections to others. A study done in hardwood and leather or a plastic computer work station or dorm desk piled with the bric-a-brac of hasty daily student life may be your ideal. Any reasonable writing setting is fine as long as it works for you.

Competing Sometimes

Like many other resources in our increasingly crowded world, good writing places are more often created than discovered. In a time of shrinking college budgets, libraries close earlier, student centers are opened for more non-campus functions, and computer labs grow more slowly. Although much writing can be done in classroom workshops, in residence halls, and at home, you have to be assertive about finding other places with the special features you require.

The only tip I can give is to start your search early in the term: learn the computer lab hours, the nights the student center has open study rooms, the coziest nooks in the library, and the quietest all-night coffee shop.

Finding and making the right places to write is not always easy. But like any other aspect of writing, once you get into the habit of making places and hardware work for you, the writing gets done.

Chapter 10

Making Writing Time

Often, more pressing than finding places to write is finding and making time. The answer is not as simple as the popular notion one is a "morning person" or a "night person" but of making writing times a flexible and integral part of your daily campus routine. If time is a commodity, then it is at a premium in your college student life. Like any commodity, time has to be discovered, acquired, and used wisely. Because the hours of the day are invisible, they are often ignored until assignment deadlines become all too obvious. Then, in the rush like one-night-stand writing, time is used to get the job done but also to make oneself uncomfortable, unsociable, and unaware of learning opportunities.

Over the years, professional writers and students alike have expressed their preferences for what they consider to be "prime" writing times. With possibly one exception discussed below, there is no consensus, no formula about personality types corresponding to time of day or day of week. But even if patterns are not clear, a range of options, discussed in this chapter, exists that can be used to stimulate your thinking in several directions.

Peeking at the Pros

I cannot say when most professional writers do their work. On the basis of reading interviews, I find that the range of response goes from "whenever" to "all the time." Certainly professional writers think about their craft when they aren't in the act of writing, but this act of putting words to paper is done to suite the schedule of the individual. Edgar Allen Poe is said to have written deep into the night; one contemporary writer says if his writing isn't done for the day at nine in the morning, it's not going to be done.

Most professional writers I have talked to seem to prefer either the early morning (not a popular alternative among first-year college writers the last time I checked) or latenight to do the physical act of writing. Perhaps these are quietest times when everybody leaves them alone or when they think the best.

Finding the Time

Mostly I don't. At least not with anything that resembles regularity. In the best of all possible worlds, I, like some professional writers, prefer to do my writing in the early morning before the phone rings, while I'm still in my robe, before I've eaten breakfast. I'll spare the tripe about "a new day," "fresh morning air," and "the quiet of dawn." I just happen to write better and longer in the early hours before the other responsibilities of the day squeeze out of me the will and concentration to write.

Much of this book, my dissertation before that, and the academic papers before and since were written at odd hours during the day, in stolen minutes and hours between classes, while waiting for students to visit my office, while slugging down a cup of something hot in a cafe. It was written only when free time in my schedule in teaching, reading, parenting, and other responsibilities allowed— even vacations during the academic year. There has been no rhythm to it, only the doggedness of making meaningful marks on paper when I could.

When my students ask me about my writing times, I am careful to separate the physical act of writing from the other times when I am thinking about or planning a piece of writing. Let me illustrate. About the time I finished the first draft of this book I gave a paper about some of the issues I encountered writing it. Most of the ideas or at least the general plan for the paper came to me one night while I was driving to teach my out-of-town class two months prior to my presentation. Off and on until the night of the presentation, I worked on the word processor expanding and refining the meaning. The results of my reading and thinking erupted in a moment behind the wheel when I couldn't physically write. The act of writing happened in the periods between other normal activities.

The moment that I discovered the idea was as productive as it was unexpected.

The point of all this is that I can empathize with your hectic and shifting academic and social responsibilities and desires. However, you must not hesitate to note the ideas when they come to you and you should realize your advantages especially if you are without spouse, children, mortgage, full-time job, etc.

College life gives us lots to do. But in those times when the action wanes, when you find yourself standing in a long line at the cashier's office, or performing some monotonous job, your mind does not have to shut off. Students have told me that many of their best writing ideas come to them when they are doing something completely unrelated to writing. They recognize the importance of the moment and get to writing as soon as they have their favorite hardware in hand.

Glancing at Some Usual Writing Schedules

The simplest one is any time you want.

As mentioned in the last chapter, when I was a residence hall director, any time of any day I saw students alone in empty classrooms, hallways, or fireplace lounge writing. Spread out in these places with books, paper, and pen or electronic typewriter, they were writing. I often noticed the activity these students practiced all day and evening, going alone and with their friends. These writing times were theirs.

Some students who organize their affairs over a number of days prefer the time-block approach in which they discipline themselves to write during a period they plan in advance. In that arbitrary hour or so between classes or after work, they spread out their stuff in a convenient place with the noise of campus around them, finishing their papers a bit at a time, according to plan, toward the due date.

In a less constrained way, many students just seem to write whenever the spirit moves them. Without a schedule, they move toward their goal, sometimes typing a word or two, sometimes word-processing for hours in their own space bubble of solitude. Although there may be no obvious time frame, they finish their work in plenty of time.

An all-too-familiar approach is the unplanned one-night-stand session. Usually this masochism, the least productive way to write, results from the panic of an imminent deadline. To try to do your essay in one sitting especially late at night just before the deadline, almost guarantees you will learn little from the experience except how much coffee you can stomach. It's tough to do good thinking late, under pressure, and chemically altered. It's hard on your health, fogs your brain, and disturbs the sleep of others. I've been there. I was there for a long time. Try not to do it often. Better yet, just don't do it.

WRITER'S MIRROR 10.1

Describe your usual writing schedule capturing the feeling that is usually associated with it.

_____

_____

_____

_____

_____

_____

Scheduling the Right One for You

Now consider an option different from the mobile, the regimented, inspired, and panicked.

Ask yourself how often some of your best writing ideas came to you when you weren't writing at your desk or in the library. My guess is your answer is "Often!" Those are valuable writing times, too, when you can be productive without making a big deal out of it. Ideally you will take a moment from whatever you are doing to jot your ideas into your writer's notebook or the back of your hand. But if you are doing something else that makes notetaking impossible (like driving) then force yourself to remember or repeat aloud your ideas until you get back to your desk.

By taking advantage of these seemingly odd times, you can get ahead of the game to capture your best ideas, to save time when you are hunkered in for typing your paper.

You may ask, "But what about drafting and polishing my writing? Making notes and drawing a few arrows on scratch paper is one thing, but what about writing the essay?" A large part of the answer for you has already been answered in the earlier chapters as you have been organizing yourself for writing.

In terms of time itself, no substitutes exist for these: starting early, writing when you're most ready, and finding where writing fits in the rest of your life.

Starting early is always sound—and often misunderstood—advice. Students often equate an early start writing with beginning as soon as the assignment is given, or getting up with the sun, or making writing the first homework done each day. In its place, any of these "early starts" may work for you. However, consider "early" in the context of all the things you have to do. I find that in writing an early start has no advantage in itself if I have nothing to write. More important is getting started when you can hold the string of your ideas once you begin.

As in any study or practice of art, time has a psychological reality as well as one on the face of your digital clock-radio. The writer must keep an idea psychologically alive to know where it came from, where it's been, and where it's going. If you have two weeks to write an essay, beginning it at once makes a lot of sense if you can hold it in your mind as you add to it each day, writing and talking to others about it. Beginning a week before it's due makes more sense if you cannot devote yourself to it beforehand because of tests, reading in other courses, work, or personal issues. Once your mind is more clear, you should proceed at once, writing in the time that is available.

Writing when you're most ready sometimes has little to do with outside commitments. Like with so many other parts of life, a writer has to feel that the time is right. In simple terms, this readiness implies having enough subject matter to begin and a favorable disposition.

If you're like many other students, you have done your school writing only when you've had to; over time you may associate writing with a feeling of tension. Consider another way: Think about getting up for writing the same way you would for a sport. Just as you may get "psyched" for a fast game of volleyball, you can get psyched to write. You know, however, when you're ready to jog onto the court; you can develop a sense, too, of when you're ready to slip in front of the keyboard. If the necessary research and reflection is well along, if you're alert, if you're ready to share ideas, then you're probably ready to write.

You may not feel you are a "natural" writer—few students do—so you may have to think about how writing and the idea of you're being a writer fit into your life. This fit can happen in several ways. One is purely mechanical: if it's between 7 and 9 Monday night, then that's writing time. Another way is that writing gets shoehorned in anywhere it can after or around other matters. A third way is to make some parts of writing go on along with other activities.

Now perhaps is the time to consider another fit: that writing can and should be an important part of your growing mental life and needs to be a priority. One of the most difficult problems I have created for myself is resolving the contradiction between writing being important for me and finding time to do it. For me, something had to give, to be moved out of my life to spend time as a writer. In my case the someTHING was actually a collection of some THINGS, but I have given up nothing necessary to the idea of who I am. I teach, read, enjoy the outdoors, and spend time with the people close to me. Writing may impinge on these other parts of life but has never overwhelmed them.

In your case, perhaps you are adapting to campus life so it is not easy to tell what is going to be important or not. My advice is to spend some time writing for your classes each day outside of classtime. Unless you're on a military-style or, alternatively, a living-for-the-day schedule, non-classtime learning life evolves along with your other activities and should come first to the degree that you want to succeed.

WRITER'S MIRROR 10.2

Show some ways you can modify your usual writing schedule to help you write better with less anxiety.

_____
_____
_____
_____
_____
_____

Probably the one idea I want to leave you with at the end of this chapter is that you have to master time. Institutions—colleges included—create time structures that serve institutional purposes and institutional convenience. If you have ever had trouble registering for classes that fit your schedule, have had to solve an impossible math problem set, or faced a tough final exam schedule, you *know* what I mean.

As a student in a first-year college writing class, you can master time by recognizing writing and thinking as actions that go along as you will them to. Often students tell me something like, "I'm sure I'll get my paper done. After all, I have two WEEKS." I ask them to think instead about the HOURS they have available during those two weeks. After attending other classes, doing homework, commuting, eating, sleeping, and goofing off, suddenly time seems much shorter.

We as writers master time by using the few minutes here and there as well as the hours we must budget. By doing so, we place more time under our control and less under the institution, the amusements of popular culture, and the built-in trap of our own forgetfulness and procrastination. Long after college is over, the habits of using time to think, to talk about important ideas, and to jot notes to yourself may serve you better than any formal "lesson" from your writing course.

Chapter 11

Choosing Writing Hardware

The tools you write with, whether a pencil stub or a microcomputer, can affect your writing performance and self-perception. In the almost 21st century, you as a student have a greater range of writing technology available than ever before. Some of you have been pecking on word processors since grade school, others have used typewriters—electronic and manual, and others feel most comfortable rolling along with a ballpoint pen. The purpose of this chapter is not to promote one technology over another, but to show how they can complement one another.

High tech alone cannot make you a better writer. Shakespeare wrote with a quill; Hemingway often with a portable typewriter. While reading this chapter, consider the range of usually taken-for-granted writing hardware—notebook paper, ballpoints, typewriters, microcomputers, etc. Although it is generally agreed high tech gear can provide a certain edge in terms of saving time and increasing ease of production of the final paper, high tech writing hardware can have disadvantages in certain writing situations. The writer must know how to use high tech to advantage.

Recollecting Low Tech

Until I bought a computer in graduate school six or seven years ago, I had always been a pen-preliminary-drafts-manual-typewriter-final-draft kind of guy. I would write out my rough drafts in long hand—usually in fountain pen because of its dark line—leaving every other line on my notebook paper blank. When I was all done with that, I went back through with a magic marker blotting out every mistake and crummy construction I could find. Then I would rewrite as necessary, sometimes scissoring out whole sections and/or taping new text over the old. At this point I moved this ragged pile to the typewriter, making substantial alterations to my text at the keyboard and glancing occasionally at the dictionary.

Once I knew a student who composed EVERYTHING on the typewriter, sometimes typing only one draft. I was amazed he went oh so slowly composing his building blocks of meaning so he would not have to change a single word he typed. Until he dropped out of college, his method worked for him.

Both of these low tech approaches had their time, but there is no reason for you to be stuck in the past.

Living in the Word Processing Present

As I am writing now, I recall other methods students use to write but of course the biggest technological change in college writing—and writing everywhere—has been the advent of the microcomputer. Now it is possible to write a whole essay without touching paper from start until finish when you tear the final paper out of the printer. I have become addicted—yes, addicted—to these machines but this addiction is shared by many. My pen and paper method went out years ago. I wrote my 247-page dissertation while I was teaching myself word processing (a learning approach I do not recommend if you want your paper done in a timely fashion). If I had had spelling and grammar checking software at the time, I probably would have used them.

Composing on a word processor can quite simply turn you into an industry. Two years ago I asked one of my basic composition students what steps he used in writing. He listed four: (1) typing his paper on his computer, (2) running spell check software, (3) running his grammar check software, and (4) printing his finished paper. A marvelous process it seemed, except he had taken himself out of the composition loop! One other problem was that his papers were usually painstakingly correct but needed to acknowledge purpose, context, and audience. High tech, in this case, worked against the student because he excluded some other important kinds of work a writer should do.

WRITER'S MIRROR 11.1   What writing hardware do you use? How does it work for you?

Using High Tech with Caution

Current technology promises miracles in the years to come—faster and smaller machines, foolproof software, etc. But I would like to propose a more hands- and mind-on approach to using the writing hardware and software available to you.

Throughout this book, I have stressed the importance of writers working (1) with one another, (2) in a variety of circumstances that blend with their everyday lives, (3) in control at different times, and (4) for greater learning. Electronic technology, if we let it, can short-circuit at least three of these four.

Think about it: most word processing and microcomputer work for that matter is largely solitary. True, a friend or teacher can lean over, but like watching television, you look at and manipulate the controls but not really talk to each other. The emphasis is often on what the machine can do.

Second, working exclusively on a word processor ties you closely to a writing time and place, a situation similar to a turn-of-the-century shop. If you have a computer, especially a laptop, you can write where you want to. But if you don't own one, you are restricted not only to sometimes crowded lab but to its schedule as well.

Working with computers can help us to use time wisely in the early stages of composition; however, we sometimes get caught up in the "needs" of the machine, technical glitches, and distractions of word count, formatting, and disk space.

Last, in later stages of writing, of revision, minor and major, computer writers are tempted to work on only the parts of the text that instructors and peers have pointed out to them. Since the essay is on disk, it can be printed after making just a few changes. Writing and revising with my pre-microcomputer method, I had to retype the whole thing. Although this seems "inefficient" today, it was more EFFECTIVE because it forced me to reread and RECONSIDER the whole paper. The result was often many more improvements in the whole text.

Using Low Tech and High Tech Together

Don't get me wrong: wordprocessing is a boon to writers everywhere speeding up production, providing online help, and taking the drudgery out of preparing deadline drafts. The net result should be more time to experiment with compositions and to improve one's general writing ability. Do beware how word processing can seduce you away from critical thinking, collaborating with others, and asking your instructor important critical questions.

Balance composing on the computer with asking the right questions and collaborating with others. Each stage of your writing has hardware appropriate to it. If you have read the previous chapters, you have a good idea of my own approach. But for yourself, consider ways to work that can maximize collaborative learning while writing.

Sometimes the best technology to begin with is none at all; simply use your five senses, your mind, and gift of speech respectively to observe, reflect on, and talk about the issues in your world. Even a simple piece of chalk needs to be guided with intelligence by human hand to spell out meaning.

For times when you just get an idea or have the urge to scribble, any lowtech pen, or marker is fine. Just about any good idea you have begins with a single line notation on a napkin or in a notebook. Jack Kerouac, the vagrant beat novelist of the American 1950s always carried a cheap notebook in his jeans pocket so he could write down ideas that came to him in jazz joints, at parties, and on the road.

Computers are great when you're ready to start drafting your work, when you are ready to sit down, focus, take the plunge. But even after you have started processing, it's a good idea to get out of the chair to read your essay away from the hum of the computer, to sit outside or in your den and scribble on it again with your felt tip pen finding places to improve meaning.

I have difficulty proofreading a computer screen—maybe I watched too many Saturday morning cartoons too close to the TV when I was a kid. Who knows? What I do know is that my proofreading is oh-so-much better when I have my writing on a leaf of paper in front of me. I also look forward to getting away from my computer desk at the office to revise at home.

Production of the final draft is of course slick with a computer. Computer printers are quick once a print command is given. A letter-quality dot-matrix printer or laser printer on 20-lb. micro-perf paper can make even a one-night-stand writing job look great at arm's length. Saved on a floppy disk or in a hard drive, your writing is always available for later production and further revision.

WRITER'S MIRROR 11.2

What mix of writing hardware works best for your various stages of writing? Explain why.

_____

_____

_____

_____

_____

_____

I have tried to make the case for a range of writing technologies showing how various ones can be used to help you work better independently, collaboratively, and learnedly. You will have to use writing hardware in ways best suited to needs, campus community, and budget. But never feel that high tech or low tech is the only way to go at every stage. Leave your writing process open so you don't lock yourself away from hardware options appropriate to your needs.

Chapter 12

Remembering Your Writing

You don't have to reinvent the wheel in your college writing class nor will you have to after you finish it. Although your teacher may have specific requirements for essays, you already have a wealth of language knowledge, writing knowledge from school, and a lifetime of listening, talking, reading, and writing. Not only behind you but ahead as well. Also, you should feel more willing to write with others, giving and seeking help. Of course implied in all of this is the community role writing plays in life—yours and the people around you.

This last chapter will discuss the importance of recalling it all for profitable use in your future classes and for writing needs later.

Reflecting on Our Guardian Language

As a writing student, you may be haunted and not even know it. As I said in Chapter 8, former teachers, parents, and school buddies may live inside of you as ghosts, reminding you of ways to be a writer. Sometimes these ghosts are benign, sometimes less so. Over the years students have said that they have been told by English teachers who meant well that they should never ask a question in an essay.

A fellow teacher once said to me that she had noticed that several students in her class who, incidentally, came from the same high school, always began their essays with the phrase, "In the world today. . . ." She learned that all these students had had the same teacher and that this phrase, they had been told, was sure to show a relationship between whatever topic they wrote about and current events.

Most of our knowledge about literacy we would like to think is useful and can be used to build yet greater skill. Basic sentence structure, paragraph organization, punctuation, spelling, word choice, consistency of tone, etc., etc. are elements we master to varying degrees, and it is this knowledge you bring into your writing classrooms and workshops.

However, we cannot always find a source for this kind of knowledge; seldom, if ever, do we have to. Think about it a minute: How often is it that we can recall where we learned a bit of general knowledge? When did you learn to use a period? When did the idea of a sentence become more or less automatic? Who guided you through your first paragraphs? I can't say who, when, where, or how I learned these things. I remember how these became refined in my later writing, but all the sources of that early knowledge about written language are gone.

Maybe some came from my mother. Much of it came from the public schools I attended, but how could I ever reassemble how I learned the fundamentals of written speech?

The truth is I can't and probably shouldn't spend too much time on it—and you shouldn't either. But it may be good to recall from time to time that our language facility came from a group of human beings or the voices and printed words that were close to us. This recollection can be a useful step in understanding our difficulties and triumphs in first-year comp.

What is important for you now is to identify for yourself where you have come from as a writer to help you and your fellows become better writers, and to talk to your writing classmates and teacher about the "rules" of your writing that may stand in the way of your making further progress.

Consider: As in the example above do you cling to some ideas about writing you cannot defend EXCEPT maybe you vaguely remember a teacher told you years ago you should or shouldn't do a certain thing? Does this sound familiar: "The topic sentence of a paragraph must always come first!"

Writing is seldom an all-or-nothing proposition. Although it is true we should generally follow conventions of written English, the creative modification of these rules occurs often. You should recognize which patterns help and which hurt your writing in a given context. The only way you will learn this is writing then talking it out with your teacher and classmates.

You may get discouraged though. Perhaps you will make an honest effort to "get a handle" on your past writing experience. You begin to get a glimmer of how your past teachers and neighborhood have affected your writing ability. You begin to talk about these influences and put into practice the fundamentals you missed and the inventiveness you were previously afraid of (I can begin a sentence with "And!" "Not every paragraph needs a concluding sentence!") But then suppose no one really seems to notice or care or, even worse, tells you it is still all wrong?

So what do you do with it? Sometimes it all seems like a waste because your composition teacher wants you to write "his way." You were back trying to play the game of finding out "what the teacher wants."

Don't despair.

One marvelous quality about writing is its complexity, a complexity that defies stylistic uniformity. When a teacher says to write his way, there is still a wide range acceptable writing; no reasonable instructor will demand the writing of every student be the same.

What is important is to look at what you have gained. Written language may no longer be invisible to you—no longer an unknown and unchangeable thing.

You see that your knowledge came from somewhere, sometime, probably many places at many times. You know that this knowledge can be improved. You know that this new knowledge can be applied.

No writing class has all the answers. The one you presently have is another in the string of those who believe that she is doing a professional job of helping you write. At the end of this course you can say that this teacher, like the others before, promoted her "way" and that you have gained something. But you should feel confident enough that you can consciously reject some of it too. In particular that anyone's commands or advice about writing is law. In the end, you teach yourself to consider the various ideas over the years and make your own laws about your writing—smart enough to get good grades, tough enough to make better decisions each time you write.

WRITER'S MIRROR 12.1

When is it useful to remember past writing experiences?

_____

_____

_____

_____

_____

_____

Beginning Memory Now

Now that you are in college, you are in a better position to make sense out of your language and develop personally logical systems for understanding how it can work for you.

In the course of the term, you will write a number of papers, talk to your teacher and classmates, and think more closely about the ways you are using language. During the course, with the aid of your writer's notebook and essays, you should become clear about the strengths and weaknesses in your writing. Knowledge like this should become a part of store of learning that is always subject to change, improvement, and all too often loss.

When I taught at a university that had a three-term composition requirement, I was amazed and sad at the amount of writing skill my students lost during the ten-day quarter breaks. My A- students would return writing C+ papers. I have never understood this problem, one that persists today.

Many colleges have an upper division writing course and/or a writing proficiency exam for a graduation requirement. Even without these requirements, staying in touch with your writing skill should be a priority. Seeing the connection between your comp course and the writing you will do later is a step. Not all of your college courses have writing requirements, so the talent you've polished in comp gets tarnished quickly without practice.

Once you realize that after intro comp that you will have to be writer for your college career and for life, it may be good to keep this realization fresh. One way to do this of course is to use writing more after your composition class than you did before. Keeping skills sharp by writing when you tried to avoid it before is a good policy: write letters, take more careful class notes, and write out study guides for exams. Critically reading your textbooks not just for content but for style helps, too. There's nothing wrong with saying, "I would write this sentence this way!" while reading your poly sci. Keeping a scrapbook of newspaper and magazine articles relevant to your field keeps you word-aware of the uses of writing in your field.

In the end you understand that there is more than just writing skills involved. The reading we do is as important for models of writing as it is for learning subjects. Remembering what we learn and applying it during and after a composition course prepares us for future literacy demands that we can barely guess right now.

When we were kids, our parents would demand, "Where did you hear that?!" when we said something they didn't like. Usually when we are young the assumption is that what we think and say comes from our listening environment. When we're in high school and later, people just as often ask "Where did you read that?!" The message of this of course is that we become readers as we mature because we have to be in school, on the job, and in complicated leisure.

What may be just as important is that we can be more conscious of CHANGES in our speech and writing. In college, we are asked more often than ever to know the sources of our ideas. It is just as reasonable to expect to know where we find the models for our writing.

The advantages of this reflection may not be apparent at once, but such knowledge can help us to be more honest writers as we try to improve in our writing courses. As we go through the course, we will become more proficient, building on past learning, past strengths. In discarding less successful writing strategies, we may recall were we "picked up" our writing knowledge and know how we are changing now. The corrections of our instructor, reading from textbooks and elsewhere, friendly advice from friends can all make our writing better—especially if we recall the interpersonal moments that bring about that learning.

I was in my mid-twenties before a classmate pointed out that "there's a pa, not a pe, in 'separate'." In writing even later, I was reminded by a professor that a paragraph needs to be written so the reader can logically follow. Now when I write, these episodes stay with me; I even use them as examples for my students. When I write, I am aware of the sea of voices whispering their advice to me over the years.

I once read about a guide in colonial Africa who carried neither rifle, knife, nor any other of the accessories of his profession yet he was remarkably successful. In our literacy lives, the fewer accessories we depend on can be enabling. We know that no matter how textbooks or computers define certain acts of writing, meaning is created by marks rooted in personal learning encounters of thinking and communicating together.

WRITER'S MIRROR 12.2

What will you take out of this writing class that you have learned from your instructor, classmates, and others?

_____

_____

_____

_____

_____

_____

Fewer Words to Close

So. That's all there is to it. Right? Wrong.

I wish I could say, "There you have it. Now you're a writer!" But that would be plainly dishonest. If you are reading this at the end of the writing course, you may be experiencing relief, that yes, one way or another, you made it through composition. Actually, you may have little writing to do from now on in the rest of your college career except for a nasty junior-level writing course in your major or a proficiency exam. You may even enter a career where little writing will be asked.

Or you may see this course as a beginning of writing in a course of study where you will have papers, seminar reports, and presentations. Perhaps even now you anticipate graduate school in an area that requires loads of reading and writing. Maybe you will continue writing on your own with journals, submissions to campus writing contests, etc.

Regardless of what you believe might happen, you will probably not entirely escape the necessity to write and perhaps to write lengthy documents again.

Hopefully your writing course and this book have prepared you for your future writing. If not, then I hope this book has at least prepared you to meet writing with the feeling that it can be done in a way that is the best for your way of approaching literacy.

Throughout this text, I have emphasized the need for understanding yourself so that writing is not a foreign activity. You know now how to make time, give attention, and seek help when you write. You value the help of others so that you never have to face writing alone; by talking to and sharing your writing with your teacher, classmates, and friends, you are developing an idea of what it means to be "writing our way."

The intent of this book was not to make you a writer if you did not want to be one and it alone certainly didn't make you writer even if you wanted to be one. My intent was to help you be the most comfortable you could be with using written language so you can meet writing head on when it is necessary—whether that stimulus came from outside or inside of you.

All I can do now is wish you luck with your writing—and give the advice to work harder when you must and to write smarter always.